Making a Scene

Constance Wu

SCRIBNER

New York   London   Toronto   Sydney   New Delhi

Scribner
An Imprint of Simon & Schuster, Inc.
1230 Avenue of the Americas
New York, NY 10020

First Scribner hardcover edition October 2022

SCRIBNER and design are registered trademarks of The Gale Group, Inc., used under license by Simon & Schuster, Inc., the publisher of this work.

For information about special discounts for bulk purchases, please contact Simon & Schuster Special Sales at 1-866-506-1949 or business@simonandschuster.com.

The Simon & Schuster Speakers Bureau can bring authors to your live event. For more information or to book an event, contact the Simon & Schuster Speakers Bureau at 1-866-248-3049 or visit our website at www.simonspeakers.com.

Interior design by Davina Mock-Maniscalco

Manufactured in the United States of America

10   9   8   7   6   5   4   3   2   1

Library of Congress Cataloging-in-Publication Data is available.

ISBN 978-1-9821-8854-2
ISBN 978-1-9821-8856-6 (ebook)

Photographs courtesy of the author's family, except page 66, courtesy of Molly Flynn; page 92, courtesy of Becki Jones; page 156, courtesy of Kit Williamson and John Halbach; page 220, courtesy of Leah Jackson

For my daughter

Suddenly I realize
That if I stepped out of my body I would break
Into blossom.
—James Wright, "A Blessing"

Most of the names and many identifying details have been changed. Some events and conversations have been reordered and/or combined for narrative purposes.

Contents

At home in Henrico, Virginia, 1990s

Introduction

Her name was "Girl." That's it. I was in my third year of drama school at a classical acting conservatory and Girl was my character in the play *Boys' Life* by Howard Korder. It's a comedy about three young men navigating the complexities of adulthood, relationships, and scx. Because Girl was in only one scene, I wanted to make that one scene a *scene*. Girl is the lead character's (Don) one-night stand. Don picks up Girl in the record store where she works. Then he sleeps with her, cheating on his girlfriend.

The scene opens, postcoital, with Girl babbling about her dreams. Don is guilt-ridden, too filled with his inner turmoil to hear her fanciful stories.

But then she starts talking about *really* crazy shit—incest in her past, aliens eating oranges, her anorexia. She says that she lied to him about working in the record store. That she does that sometimes, she lies. That maybe she's been lying all along. Or maybe she's even lying to him about lying, because actually? She *does* work in the record store, haha! Girl starts talking so wildly that it snaps Don out of his head and into the present moment, and that's when he finally hears her.

It's a turning point in the play. We see the once light-hearted Don finally grapple with the consequences of his immaturity. Girl functions as a catalyst for Don's self-realization. That's why she's in only one scene, why she doesn't have a name. Because the play isn't about her—who it's about is right there in the title: *Boys' Life*.

I was glad to play this unnamed part. I'd already had some big leading roles during my time in drama school, so it was a relief to let the boys do the heavy lifting in this play. I got to be loose and free, knowing I wasn't responsible for carrying the story. It was so fun. I loved playing Girl.

The director and I decided that Girl was *OUT-THERE*. My costume was a ripped T-shirt and underwear. I put on a bunch of temporary tattoos and stuck fake piercings on my lips, nose, and eyebrow. I wore messy hair, excessive black eyeliner. Dark lipstick. I moved with spindly arms, loose mouth, bobbing head. I didn't sit like a lady; I sprawled. I was funny and the audience loved it! Girl was zany! And my peers delighted in seeing me, a conservative suburban Virginia girl, playing someone so out-there. Someone *with tattoos*.

I loved the response. I kept my tattoos on during non-performance days because they made me feel tough. I took pleasure in surprising people with the contrast.

One night, during a performance when I was very loose,

saying my lines and going through Girl's wild movements—something happened.

Girl spoke to me.

Her voice came into my head out of nowhere; a complete surprise. *I am more than what you're giving me*, she said.

My lines remained the same, but in the middle of that performance, everything—the way I approach acting, the way I think about people—changed. I'd written Girl off as just tattoos and black eyeliner. A crazy person. But *I am more*, she said. *Listen to me.* So, I did. And what she told me broke my heart.

Girl wasn't crazy. It's that Don wasn't listening to her. . . . She had just shared her body with him, was telling him her dreams. But he's so consumed by his own guilt, he barely registers her. That's why Girl had to get crazy, make a scene. Just to be *heard*.

———————

Growing up, I was taught to *never* make scenes. It's unbecoming. Unladylike. As a kid, I held back so much. And whenever I reached a breaking point—the accumulated feelings avalanching out of me in tears or tantrums—I found that to be ineffective too. No one heard my words; they only heard the tone and responded by saying things like "Whoa, you're intense" or "Calm down" or "Why can't you just be grateful?" Patronizing, reductive phrases that made me feel even worse. It's probably why I love theater so much: it's the only place where it felt acceptable—nay, commendable—to have big feelings.

At the end of the scene in *Boys' Life*, Don gets freaked-out and tries to leave Girl's apartment. *No, wait. Stay*, she says, realizing she's gone too far. She doesn't want him to go; what does it say about her if he leaves? She begs him, flatters him. She apologizes. She tries to have sex with him again—and *that's* the tactic that finally works. Don gets back into her bed. Girl blows out her candle, the stage goes black, and that's the end of the scene. She never appears in the play again.

Boys' Life was written in 1988, well before the world of the internet as we know it. But Girl's appearance in it feels relevant today: whenever we encounter public figures, we're often only getting one short scene—an Instagram picture, a fifteen-second video, a clickbait headline—and judging it. The scene ends, and the ensuing public commentary becomes the play. It's like how I'd initially interpreted Girl. I read her one scene and got carried away with my *own* narrative about her. . . . *She works in a record store! She has casual sex! She tells crazy stories! She is OUT-THERE! I'm gonna give her intense makeup and tattooooooooos!*

But then she *spoke* to me and I finally listened—*really* listened—to her. I stopped thinking of her as a girl making a scene, and started thinking about the scenes that made the girl. When I did that, when I took the time to look deeper, it changed my life and my craft for the better.

The stories in this book are memories of the people and events that have shaped my humanity and determined the direction of my life. Just because *Boys' Life* only gives Girl one scene in the play doesn't mean *we* have to. Her story doesn't end when the scene ends. She has a future. She has a history. That's what I'm trying to do with this book. To tell the story of my own inner Girl, ya know? Give her a few more scenes.

In New York City, 2006

Lucky Bucks

My heart dropped down to the bottom of my feet. The only other time I'd had that feeling was when my dad was very sick, and I saw him collapse because he couldn't breathe. As his airway constricted, his eyes glazed in panic. His arms reached out around him as if for balance, for air, for anything at all, until he fell to the floor. Terror and love and helplessness flooded every cell of my body; a feeling as dull as underwater voices and sharp as a needle piercing your chest. And when I first saw Rob, when my heart dropped to the bottom of my feet again, it was a lot like that, but *good.*

Years later, Rob would admit to me that when he first saw me, he felt all the air leaving his lungs. That I took his breath away. Not because I was some hot thang, but because I was a surprise. He hadn't expected me.

Because I came in the wrong entrance. It was my first day of training as a waitress at a trendy New York restaurant called XYZ. Rob was the maître d', so he stood at the front of the restaurant, behind the host stand. I did everything wrong that day. They told me that trainees should arrive wearing black. My previous waitressing job had been at at a hip cocktail bar in Union Square, where the dress code was: something sexy, but NO denim. So, I took the "wear black" directive as the same, and I wore a cute strapless black minidress. Trainees and staff were supposed to enter through the service door, but I didn't know that, so I walked straight through the front door of the restaurant in my black mini-dress. That's when Rob looked up and I saw him and my heart dropped and he lost his breath. We both hid it, recovering quickly, becoming overly casual.

"Hi, where do I go?" I asked.

"Go?" he said, puzzled, not realizing I was a trainee.

"Oh, I'm a new waitress? I'm training today?" He looked at my dress, gave me a practiced, cool smile, and motioned to the back corner of the restaurant, where a group of trainees was gathered. They were all wearing formal black button-up shirts, pressed black slacks, and black dress shoes. My face turned bright red. Stupid minidress. They should have been more specific when they said wear black! But they let me train anyway, and I felt embarrassed the whole shift.

It was a large restaurant, and for the first month or so Rob and I didn't interact much. But of course I was aware of Rob; everybody talked about him. As maître d', who kinda ran the restaurant, he was the gatekeeper to the trendiest spot in town. Celebrities and finance bros gave him green handshakes to be sat immediately, floating right past fuming diners waiting for tables they'd had reservations for for months. Usually tourists, they'd protest, and it often got heated. But even when customers were screaming in his face, he always kept his cool. He was tall and lean with sculpted features, golden skin. He wore black Converse sneakers, blue jeans, and threadbare vintage T-shirts in muted colors that hung on his body just right. Somehow these clothes looked appropriate on him even though everyone else was in uniform. It was powerful and alluring to watch him at work—his casualness, the way he stood, hip cocked to the side, one foot on top of the other as he scanned the reservation screen. The way he'd lightly tell the hostesses what section to seat. Of course, that heart-falling-to-feet feeling had meant something. But I brushed it off as physical attraction. And when I heard, through waitresses' whispers, that he was a model, I *really* wrote him off. *No way*, I thought. *I date smart people, deep people.* So Rob was a no-go. He was a model, he ran the restaurant, and *everybody* wanted him. I rolled my eyes—just another hot person in a city of hot people. Nothing special.

Sara was the one who made it happen. Sara was one of my first friends at XYZ. She was a waitress and an aspiring singer. She was thick, sexy, and confident. She had an Afro and pronounced her name "saw-raw," trilling the *r*. She loved astrology and crystals. I wasn't into that kind of stuff, but when Sara talked about it, I liked to listen.

One shift, as we were sneaking peanut butter cookies in one of the private party rooms, she started grilling me about boys. I got embarrassed, embarrassed about being single. Sara thought this was nothing to be ashamed of. Then she said, "You need to go talk to Robert. Something is going to happen there."

I scoffed "Rob? The maître d'? For real? Ha. No way."

She continued eating her cookie, ignoring my dismissive laughter. "The way he looks at you, Constance."

My face flushed with heat. "He looks at everyone like that," I stammered. "He's a model. It's posing. That's what models do."

She stared at me like I was stupid. Then she said, "Okay, so the way he tries to *not* look at you."

I hadn't spoken to him since that first day of training. She insisted I go talk to him. I was so scared I felt like hiding in a corner but I obeyed Sara because you *had* to obey Sara. I put down my peanut butter cookie and went to find him. It was a quiet time at the restaurant, 4:00 p.m., after the lunch crowd had cleared and before the dinner service. The servers were setting tables, folding napkins, polishing wineglasses. The afternoon light slanted onto the floor, casting shadows in the denim folds of Rob's blue jeans as he stood at the host podium, where he organized the reservations and seating charts for the evening. My heart started racing. He was so hot.

He was reading a book. Perfect. I read lots of books. I walked up to him and casually asked what he was reading. It was a psychology textbook, he explained, because that's what he was studying in grad school.

"Oh, but everyone said you're a *model*." I rolled my eyes, teasing him.

He smiled. "I was," he said. "But not anymore."

"Why not?"

He closed his book and considered me. "I guess it's sort of an impermanent thing, you know?"

"Well . . . isn't everything?" I responded with a shrug. I saw something catch in his throat as I flashed a sly smile, turned on a dime, and walked away, leaving him speechless. I felt his eyes and his speechlessness behind me. Holy SHIT! How had I done that? I had never done that before! Where the hell had that confidence come from? It was the first time I felt like I had enchanted a man. And *this* man?! It was a power that I didn't know I could possibly have over someone.

Maybe a week after that, he asked if he could take me out to lunch sometime.

Dinner, I said.

Deal.

Our first date was at an awful restaurant. Stainless steel decor and orange mood lighting, it was like Italian-Japanese-Mexican-Texan-farm-to-table fusion. (My fault, I chose it.) But the conversation was exhilarating. I ordered a pomegranate cocktail that was disgusting but strong. I drank it all, sinking into a warm daze of discovery and excitement. After dinner, we walked around the city for hours, aimless, just talking. Time disappeared. At some point, we started holding hands. Eventually we ended up in this little park on the west side, a few blocks from the Hudson River. There was a playground that had frog sculpture things for kids. We sat on a nearby bench and laughed at them like *what even are these frogs?* and it was there by the frogs that he first kissed me, filling my body with ache.

First it was *like*—we really liked each other. We spent every night together. Staying up late, talking by candlelight about philosophy and the meaning of life. Former loves and what we'd learned from them. Faith, family. Our dreams and fears. We had a connection that felt cosmic. For the first few months, we often talked all night, forgetting time. We were never even drunk or high, except on each other.

Then it was *laughter*. Fooling around. After sex we'd both be so happy it made us silly. Him doing funny little naked dances. Me falling over giggling as I watched his dick swinging along with his dance moves. We once played this prank at a restaurant where we staged a fake argument, just to make a scene, amplifying the fight until people were looking at us. I stormed out of the restaurant in a pretend fury. He ran after me, and we both collapsed in laughter on the sidewalk, delighted by our own game, knowing that everyone in the restaurant was talking about that crazy fight they just witnessed. We had a plan to go to the fanciest restaurant in the city and order a nice craft beer, then pull his beer bong out of my purse and bong it in the middle of the restaurant. We never actually did that, but we did lots of similar little games. Dumb stuff like that was funny to us. Looking back, it sounds annoying and attention-seeking. And it *was*—we were calling attention to our joy so that others might share in it. In a naive way, we thought our pranks and outbursts were gifts to the world.

We had sex that was both loving and great fucking. We experimented and weren't afraid or embarrassed to ask for what we needed, to try different things. We ate cookies in bed. Big cookies from a brand called Nana's that we bought at Westerly Market around the corner from his apartment. We fell asleep holding each other and woke up that way too.

And finally it was *love*. It happened quite naturally. One late night, he told me to put my bare chest on top of his so we could feel our hearts beating together, so I did, and we really did feel each other's heartbeats. It was a pleasure so delicate and fine, like a baby feeling the gentle brush of a feather on her eyelids for the first time, blinking and smiling at the new sensation. And while we were there, looking at each other, feeling each other's heartbeats, we said "I love you" for the first time. We said it at the exact same second.

This sounds unbelievable, but sometimes we even dreamed the same dreams.

We still worked at XYZ together. He told me how sometimes, when he watched me talking to a table or serving a customer a drink, he'd feel so much insane love for me that he was overwhelmed with the urge to run and crash into me, like a damn linebacker. He never actually did it, but sometimes I'd glance up at him from my table and I could see it in his eyes. Like we both knew. Later we marveled at and theorized about that feeling. About how that's what love was, wasn't it? That's why sex was what it was, we thought. You felt so wild about a person that you wanted to literally meld into each other. It was a need so strong it hurt. Painful that we had to live our lives in separate bodies.

His job as maître d' required him to stay at the podium the whole shift, surrounded by pretty hostesses, but I was never jealous because they were my friends. Except for one, Penelope, who didn't even work there anymore! When she came into the restaurant to visit, one of the hostesses told me she and Rob had made out a few times. While I wasn't threatened, I was wildly jealous of her. She was blond and gorgeous and tall and went to Princeton. I knew Rob was impressed by intelligence. Even though I was smart, I was short and dark and had a degree from a performing arts college. Penelope's visit brought out the worst in both of us—I was too naive then to know that it was uncool for a woman to be jealous and I talked openly about it. Rob told me that it actually made him feel good in a weird way, that I was possessive of him. A pompous sentiment, but he was too naive to censor it. There wasn't any pretense. We just said what we felt and got mad or sad or irrational and forgave each other and somehow fell deeper in love because of it.

At work one of Rob's duties was to give the hostesses little notes for them to deliver to the server. Those notes were called VIP dupes but they weren't just for VIPs; sometimes they were special customer requests: "Birthday candle for man at table 12," "Pre-authorized credit card at table 41," "Peanut allergy for child at table 27," etc. Most of the tables didn't require VIP dupes, so you usually only got two or three dupes a night. But I got them all night, for every table. Whenever Rob sent a hostess to my section of the restaurant, he gave her a VIP dupe to pass on to me. They were usually little love notes or silly drawings of stick figures with dicks. Sometimes "I LOVE YOU!!!!!!!!!!!!!" followed by a second dupe that continued "!!!!!!!!!!!" Every VIP dupe I got from Rob flooded me with joy. It's funny how reading those little slips of paper are some of my happiest memories. Just a little piece of paper. One time, he sent a hostess to my section with a VIP dupe attached to a plastic bag. Sometimes a guest would bring their own bottle of wine or a birthday cake, so I assumed that's what was in the bag. But as soon as I saw the look on the hostess's face I knew that something was up.

Barely able to contain her laughter, she handed me the bag. "This is from Rob," she said. I opened it, stuck my hand in, and pulled out . . . one of his shoes! The hostess couldn't hold it in anymore and we both burst out laughing. I looked at him from across the restaurant and there he was, cool as a cucumber, talking to a customer, knowing I was watching. I looked at his feet, and sure enough, there was his shoeless, socked foot stacked on top of his standing foot behind the podium. I told the hostess I was keeping the shoe for the whole shift. I watched her tell him that, and he looked over at me agape. I smiled back mischievously.

A few minutes later I gave a hostess a VIP dupe for him: "If you want your shoe back, come to the staff bathroom." I sent her off and went down there to wait. He rushed in a minute later and play-wrestled with me for the shoe, which turned into covering me with kisses. We locked the door and kissed and pushed and played and then held each other and laughed. I tried to give him a blow job but couldn't because I was also trying to hold the shoe behind my back and both of us were laughing too hard. He pulled me up and held my face in his hands, a stunned look in his eyes as he repeated, "I love you. I love you so much. You are my love." Over and over again, as if it were a discovery each time. There were tables to wait on, customers to seat. But in that moment, in a grimy staff bathroom, me in my waitressing uniform, him in one shoe with his limp dick hanging out of his pants, in that moment there was just us and the miracle of love. Of having somehow found each other.

One day, we decided to jump out of a plane. It was fall, and the leaves were orange and red. They blurred past the windows of the bus we took upstate to a skydiving ranch in New Paltz, where we strapped up, hopped in a plane, and dropped out of the sky. We went tandem with professionals. They paired your tandem skydiver according to weight, so if you were small, you had a bigger tandem guy, and if you were big, you had a smaller one. My guy was a big Russian dude who kept telling jokes. Rob's was a short, compact man who was very serious. Even though it had been Rob's idea to skydive, he was nervous. But me? I was giggling the whole time, giggling on the plane ride up into the sky and giggling as I fell out of the plane door. Somehow, I didn't have any fear. When you skydive, you don't "jump" out. You are in the plane's open doorway, holding the frame, and then you just sort of . . . let go. There's so much pressure against your body and your lips that it doesn't feel like falling; it feels hard, like a firehose blasting your whole body. Then you pull the chute and are jerked up from the firehose blast to find yourself suddenly floating, gently. Like a bubble. It was beautiful to look at the world this way. So high in the air, over the orange trees and green fields.

When we finally landed, I tried this runway technique they had taught us where you put your legs out in front of you at an angle to gently scrape the ground, to help you decelerate until you came to a stop. I was not very graceful. Rob looked more graceful, though he later said the second he put his legs out, the straps tightened around his balls, and he was like, *OW, OW, OW.* It made me laugh. We both had a juvenile sense of humor.

We went to a nearby café and got lunch and enjoyed being out of the city. By the time we got back on the bus, we were a nice kind of tired. With my head on his shoulder, and his leaned on top of mine, we fell asleep and stayed that way the whole ride back to the city.

———————

After a year or so, we started calling each other "Buck." It had started out as "Lovebug," then morphed into "Bug." It was just Bug for a while. If I had to leave earlier in the morning than he did, when I returned home I would see "BUG" spelled out on the bed with spoons and pencils and socks. We'd answer the phone and just say "Hiiii BuGGG," really hitting the G like we were gulping. We hit the G so hard that one day, Bug became Buck. And Buck stuck. I haven't called him anything but Buck since.

When we first fell in love he called it a "love seizure." That initial excitement could not be sustained, so it waned, but it was replaced by something deeper. We grew up together. We talked about our problems. We listened to each other's points of view and came to appreciate our differences. I helped him write his PhD application essays. He had great ideas, but he wasn't good at syntax and rhythm and style. I enjoyed working with him. We took care of each other when we were sick, even when it was inconvenient. We made decisions together. When we both felt that our restaurant jobs compromised the energy we could be putting toward our actual goals—his PhD in psychology and my acting career—we discussed quitting the restaurant.

I was always bad with money and in a lot of debt, but I was also a Modern Woman and Feminist who refused financial help from him or anyone else, so I decided to continue waitressing. He was good with money and had plenty saved (being a maître d' at a trendy NYC restaurant gets you a LOT of lucrative handshakes). He felt guilty for being able to quit the restaurant when I couldn't, but we talked through it and my genuine support of his choice freed him from guilt. And seeing his freedom made me happy.

Working at XYZ wasn't as fun without him around, so I got a different waitressing job that was closer to my apartment. He'd study while I was working, waiting for me to come home. At my new restaurant, they served these great tuna steaks, which they threw out if there were any left at the end of the night. They were sushi grade and really thick. Buck loved tuna steaks. So, whenever there were leftovers, I would take a couple home, where I'd sear them rare with a little salt and pepper and mustard while we caught up on each other's day. Then we'd eat, our bodies close, in front of the TV watching *So You Think You Can Dance* or *The Ultimate Fighter*, feeling like kings for having such fine food for free. Later we'd microwave cheap mini-brownies in plastic dollar-store bowls and eat them hot.

After we'd been dating awhile, my sister Helen moved to the city with her boyfriend, Mike. The four of us quickly became a friend group. Of my three sisters, she was the one I'd grown closest to in adulthood. Mike and Rob really hit it off too. When Helen and Mike went out of town, we'd dog-sit for them and stay at their nice apartment on the Upper West Side, watching their TV, eating their good snacks, and panicking over any slight thing that happened with the dog (the dog was always fine).

One New Year's Eve, Rob and I went over to their apartment. Helen made yummy hors d'oeuvres, and we played board games and drank several bottles of wine. We put a party hat on the dog that she kept shaking off. We listened to music and rolled around on the carpet, playing with the dog. It was relaxing and comfortable. We laughed about nothing and everything. Just the four of us. While I've had lots of lavish and exciting New Year's Eves, that small, casual night of board games and laughter is still the nicest one I've ever had.

When he was in his final year of grad school, Rob was nervous about the GRE. He needed a good score for his PhD applications and he wasn't great at standardized tests. The night before his GRE he was so stressed that he said he needed to be alone to focus, and I said of course and went to my own apartment. At 2:00 a.m., he called me and said, "I can't sleep. . . . I've been trying for hours. I'm so nervous. Can you come over? I need you." I jumped into a cab (that I couldn't afford) in my pajamas and sped to him. He opened the door, his eyes in a panic. I loved him so much in that moment. We sat down in the kitchen, and he unloaded his worries under the fluorescent lights. He didn't know if he was smart, he said. He really wanted to be smart. What if he didn't get into any schools?

We got in bed, he put his head on my shoulder, and I stroked his hair and talked softly about nothing until he fell asleep. He ended up doing great on the GRE. He was going to go from being a model to being a person who would have "Dr." in front of his name.

———————————

After a couple of years, I did a Shakespeare workshop where I met another guy who I probably had a connection with back then, but I was so incredibly in love with Rob I honestly didn't notice. When I was with Rob, I didn't notice anything else.

I really didn't. I didn't notice how serious he was becoming. How it was making me nervous. How he had stopped doing silly naked dances. How we didn't have pretend fake fights in restaurants just for kicks. He was on his way to being a doctor. I was still in the same place: trying to be an actress. My trajectory wasn't changing, but his was. And as I witnessed him go from cool guy model and maître d' to PhD applicant, I began to feel insecure and insufficient. That insecurity started bleeding into my acting auditions and I wasn't getting parts or even callbacks anymore. He'd ask me how my auditions went, trying to express support and interest. But I'd snap at him, embarrassed because I knew I didn't get the part.

THE SCENE: AN UNFLATTERING PORTRAIT OF THE INSECURITY THAT LEADS TO THE END.

Rob and Constance sit on a crosstown bus in Manhattan. Constance seems irritated and self-conscious. Rob senses this and attempts to cheer her up.

> ROB
>
> How'd the audition go this morning? I told
> Kurt about it. . . . He loves that show!

(Constance, suddenly scowling, snaps at him.)

> CONSTANCE
>
> Ugh, why do you have to do that?

(Rob's face falls with genuine empathy and apology as he sees her distress.)

> ROB
>
> Oh, I'm sorry, Buck. . . . What did I . . . ?

> CONSTANCE
>
> It's really fucking annoying when you ask me
> about my auditions.

> ROB
>
> Oh Buck, I'm sorry, I just know how
> important they are to you. . . .

CONSTANCE

No they're not! They're NOT fucking
important! And it's fucking annoying when
you act all "caring" about them.

ROB

. . .

CONSTANCE

Don't give me that innocent look. You don't
get it. This is just an actor's life. We do it
every day! Not every audition is a big deal.
And it's fucking annoying when you get
all excited over something that, like, I'd
already forgotten. It makes me feel like shit.
Like, when you ask me about every stupid
audition, it's really fucking shitty to do to an
actor. It's like you're putting pressure on me.
You just don't get it; don't talk to me about
stuff you don't get.

ROB

I'm really sorry, Buck.

*(Constance holds back tears by storming to the back of
the bus.)*

*(Rob doesn't quite know what to do. After a moment, he
goes to her, hat in hands, at the back of the bus.)*

ROB

Hey. Buck. I'm sorry. I'm glad you told me,
and I won't do it again. *(He tries to hold her
hand.)* Okay, Buck? I'm sorry.

*(Constance, trying not to cry and full of horrible feelings
she doesn't understand, snatches her hand away. She won't
even look at him, because she knows it will make her cry.
She can't cry. The world will fall apart if anyone sees her
cry. The only way to not cry is to stay silent and angry, so
that's what she does. When the bus reaches her stop, she
gets off and the tears finally pour out, one after another,
dropping onto the sidewalk as she buries her head and
walks away.)*

I wish I hadn't snapped at him like that. I know that it
was just because I was afraid and insecure, but I didn't realize that then. I am still sorry I took it out on him. But my
wonderful Buck, he never got defensive and never fought
back. He simply saw that I was hurting, said sorry, and took
care of me in the moment. He was a really good person.
He knew not to take things personally when I was going
through a rough time. Because, through it all—the mean-
ness, the insecurities, the feelings of aloneness and shame—
he really loved me.

And then he got into his PhD programs. One in Pennsylvania, one in DC, one in New York. He was leaning toward

Pennsylvania. I was scared that he'd be leaving, but I hid those feelings; I didn't want to taint his pride and happiness with my selfish fear. But hiding that fear meant I was hiding in general, and he started to hide too. One day he just said, "I think I'm going to Pennsylvania, and I don't want you to come with me because that wouldn't be fair to you because you're an actress and you need to be here."

Once, during the early days of our relationship, when the love was especially intense, he broke up with me for three days. It came out of nowhere. One morning, while we were cuddling in bed, he was wide-awake, but I was still half-asleep. I draped an arm over him and nestled into his shoulder, so happy I was practically cooing. As I continued dozing in his arms, he lay still and stared at the ceiling. Then, with an abrupt decisiveness, he said, "I want to break up with you. I am not ready for something this serious." His face was neutral. His manner matter-of-fact.

I was shocked awake. I didn't understand—less than a week prior, we had felt our hearts beat together and said "I love you" at the same time. I went home blurry with tears. At a loss, I called him when I got home and asked, "Are you sure?"

He was quiet for a long moment. "I . . . think so," he replied.

I became desperate. I looked up advice on how to get

your boyfriend back. Everything on the internet said that you had to act like you agreed with the breakup, pretend you weren't upset. Like you wanted whatever made him happy. And if you were happy and independent, he'd realize what he lost and come crawling back. So, I did that, writing him a long letter full of acceptance and grace, letting him go. Three days later he came back to me more wildly in love than I ever thought possible.

————————

So when he wanted to break up this time, I was armed and ready. It wasn't like when we first started dating, where I expressed all my uncomfortable feelings even when it was uncool. I really had changed. I had learned manipulation, pretense. I acted calm and logical, agreeing with him that we should split. Pretending it was the practical, loving thing to do. We decided to have a great last summer together, and then leave each other at the end of it when he went off to grad school. And if one of us met someone else, we met someone else. My heart was broken but I thought I could fake my way into not feeling.

On the outside, I was serene. But inside, I became frantic. I decided to pursue another career to impress him, to show him I could change from actress to serious student too. I'd always had an interest in linguistics; I discovered that I could apply that interest toward a career in speech-language pathology. I enrolled in post-bacc classes and applied to master's programs. I told him I was quitting acting, that I wanted to be steady and academic. Trying to prove I was independent, didn't need him. He was confused but supportive and maybe a little sad.

I began talking to a writer whose work I loved. I had corresponded with him to tell him I was a fan. We started emailing every day. He was much older than me. I constantly talked about Rob, so he knew I had a boyfriend. But when Rob was out of town visiting a grad school, the writer asked to meet up. I said okay and met him at a burger joint. I smiled hard and laughed light the whole time but inside I felt wild and desperate, my eyeline zig-zagging around the room like a pinball machine. He was nice, my heart raced. Fake laughs came out of me like hiccups. He led me out to the sidewalk on his arm. It was an overcast New York day but somehow the gray sky felt aggressively bright. When he tried to kiss me, all I could think of was Rob. . . . My heart ached for my Buck. But I was pretending, manipulating, so I kissed him back.

I told Rob as soon as he got home, hoping to ignite a jealousy and possessiveness that would make him stay, make him love me like he used to. I was sitting at the kitchen table when I told him. It was a round acrylic table from Ikea that used to be white but had become scratched and gray. He was standing by the bookshelf across the room, putting some shirts away. "Buck . . . I need to tell you something. I've been talking to this writer. . . . We went out while you were gone and . . . he kissed me," I confessed, heart pounding so hard that it felt like it could burst out of my skull. A pang of pain flashed across his face. He got quiet and something in us broke forever. We didn't talk for a bit, but he forgave me. Buck always forgave me.

And then one day, it was over. I can't remember how it happened, I really can't. I don't remember what was said or where we were. I don't know who the first person I told was. I don't know if I listened to sad music, I don't remember if I stopped eating or if I binged on ice cream, I don't remember how it felt. My mind sometimes blurs out painful experiences as an act of mercy. My breakup with Rob must have really hurt because it is gone from my memory.

When I think back on our relationship, parts of it seem cringeworthy and obnoxious. Those ridiculous faux fights in restaurants? Putting my heart on his heart and feeling them beat together and saying "I love you"? Part of me wants to groan and call it *cheesy*. Somewhere along the way, big feelings became foolish. Now that I've had more loves, I can see that what I had with Rob wasn't that special, in context. Not that extraordinary in the scope of an entire life. When I think about how we were, I think, *Ha, those young kids don't know anything! They think they're the first people to discover love.*

But we really did.

Today, Buck and I are distant friends. We're not regular presences in each other's lives, but we might send an email every few years. It took a long time for me to get over him. For several years after the breakup, I still thought it might be possible to get back together. Then, when I knew that would never happen, he was the standard to whom I compared everyone else. I've had great loves since Rob, and smaller ones too. He was once my entire life, when I was young, when I thought of him every minute of the day. But then minutes became hours became days became months became years. Today, I only think of Rob on occasion. Maybe once a year.

He is now married to a wonderful Midwestern blond woman and they have three daughters. They have a house in the suburbs with trees and a big yard. He has his PhD and is a college professor. For a while, he was a stay-at-home dad so his wife could work full-time, and I thought that was really progressive and rad of them. He has become who he wanted to be, and more.

I've always found that the turning point in recovering from a breakup is when you can look back on memories with fondness, rather than pain. And I am so fond. I feel almost proud of him. Proud that this extraordinary person was a part of my life.

The next boyfriend I had after Rob broke into my email and read all of Rob's old messages to me, because he suspected I was still in love with him. Of course I was, I will always love my Buck. I hadn't been cheating, so that boyfriend didn't find anything. But the passion of those old emails made him wild with jealousy. He made me permanently delete every email Rob ever sent to me and throw away every picture of us together. All I have now are a few photos my sister had. A poem he wrote me called "Holding All Else Constance." One of his old T-shirts. A book he gave me for Christmas one year with a note tucked inside that said:

Love, like, laughter . . . not necessarily in that order. Looking forward.

I once heard that every seven years you are biologically a completely different person, on a cellular level. Some cells, like skin cells, turn over frequently, and others, like brain cells or bone cells, last longer, years. But all of our cells eventually die and are replaced by new ones. The longest-lasting cells in a human body live around seven years, so once they're gone, once the longest-surviving cells in your body have turned over and been replaced, and your skin and hair and blood cells have already turned over many thousands of times, you are biologically a different person. No physical cells of the old you remain.

If that's true, no cellular part of the me that loved Buck remains. But somehow, love remains. Once someone touches your heart, they can't untouch it. Buck will always be my first great love, when love was still a miracle that could happen out of thin air. "I hadn't expected you," he'd said, "you were a surprise."

There's a window of time in life when you're old enough for sex to not be new, but young enough to love without fear. It's a small window. The miracle is that Rob and I found each other in that window, when I walked in the wrong door and my heart dropped to the bottom of my feet. "Something is going to happen there," Sara told me before I abandoned my peanut butter cookie and found the courage to talk to him. When he'd said, "It's sort of an impermanent thing, you know?" And I'd replied, smiling, ". . . Isn't everything?" It was like we already knew. But we fell in love anyway and I am so glad. We were so lucky.

Montana Gold

In 1997, the legal age for employment in Virginia was fifteen years old, so when I turned fifteen, I immediately looked for a job because I wanted money for new clothes. I had frugal parents, two older sisters (double hand-me-downs), and a passion for fashion—earning my own money for cool clothes was a necessity. My previous work experience had been a little babysitting, which was boring and sporadic, so I applied for a counter job at McDonald's. But they didn't hire me.

After Mickey D's rejected me, I moaned about it to my friend Jessica in chorus class. She said that the bakery where she worked was hiring and she'd put in a good word. And that's how I got a job as a cashier at Montana Gold Bread Co.

At Montana Gold we made bread the way you imagine it was made centuries ago. Even our flour was freshly milled! There was an actual flour mill, in a glass room up front for all to see, where we milled wheat into flour. All the wheat came from Montana, hence the name: Montana Gold. The bakery was owned by a friendly, wholesome couple, Rich and Sher. Rich was tall and wiry and enthusiastic. He wore glasses and had a bushy gray mustache. Sher was petite and pleasant in a way that made her whole body feel like a smile.

Montana Gold had two locations: one on Parham Road near my high school and one in downtown Carytown. Carytown was the original location and I worked there on an occasional weekend, but I mostly worked at the one near my high school. In a more suburban area, it was frequented by moms and teachers. The school's baseball coach used to come in a few times a week and buy an oatmeal-chocolate-chip cookie. Just one. My next-door neighbor Mrs. Peskin came in for focaccia every Saturday.

At Montana Gold the walls were white and plain. There was a small refrigerator with a sliding glass door that offered soda and Tropicana juices. There was coffee, of course, in plain glass pots on burners and a chalkboard that listed the daily breads. The bakery's everyday breads were honey wheat, honey white, cinnamon swirl, "CRW" (cinnamon raisin walnut), and Blue Ridge Mountain Herb. Then we had special breads that changed daily. We printed up monthly calendars with the special bread schedule, so that if you really wanted spelt or Irish soda bread or sourdough or cherry apple challah, you knew which day to come in.

Sometimes I got to do the chalkboard and I took pride in my penmanship (chalkmanship? chalkwomanship?). The chalkboard was up high on the wall, so you had to get on a ladder to do it. Other than the colored chalk, Montana Gold was clean and spare. Our uniforms were plain white T-shirts with the green "Montana Gold" emblem on the upper left corner, right over your heart. We wore jeans and bandannas and wrapped a plain white cotton apron over everything.

When I started, I just worked the cash register, but I had some other duties as well. At closing time, I cleaned the whole bakery by myself. Windexed the windows and front doors. Wiped down the counters. Oiled and scraped the wooden bread-kneading table. I washed all the dishes by hand. Swept and mopped the whole bakery, which wasn't too hard except for the flour-milling room. After I cleaned the mill room, my hair was always white, and I looked like a ghost. At the end of the closing shift, I'd cut large, refrigerated bricks of butter into halves while they were still cold and hard and easy to cut without squishing. I'd leave the halves out on a tray overnight to soften. In the morning, the butter would be soft enough to not dent your bread when spreading it with a knife, but cool enough to not melt into liquid. Creamy, easy butter.

I'd put that butter out in a large white dish next to the wooden sample board. We offered free samples of every loaf we'd be selling that day, and another of my duties was slicing samples and encouraging people to use the soft butter. I always cut really big slices for the customers. It felt good to see people eat something and enjoy it so much. People often wanted to buy the butter thinking it was super special, but it wasn't really; it was just the overnight softening that made it so good.

———

Every night, I was allowed to take a loaf home to my family. A cinnamon swirl or challah (which was described on their chalkboard as a "Jewish Egg Bread") was usually my free loaf of choice. We only sold fresh bread, so any day-old bread was given to a local soup kitchen, collected nightly by a handsome woman who looked like she had never worn makeup in her life.

As I got to know Rich and Sher and the baking team better, they let me join them at the bread-kneading table when the store was quiet. They taught me how to knead and shape bread dough. It was nice to make something with my hands, nice to feel useful. And teenage me liked listening to the team of grown-up bakers chat as they worked the dough.

There was Stuart, who was the first non-theater openly gay man I ever met (and how!). Matt, a community college student who loved cars—the kind of guy whose apartment probably had posters of cars, like, everywhere. Susan, a sweet, divorced mom with curly brown hair who later married my friend Greta's divorced dad. Todd, who loved his job and his truck so much that he combined the two—getting personalized license plates that read "MNT GOLD" on the back of his Chevy. There was Stephen, the other gay guy—dry and blasé but would have taken a bullet for his cats. Jeannie, a professional ballerina with the Richmond Ballet, which I thought was so neat. Chris, a lanky blond college art student who I had a desperate crush on. There was Jessica from chorus, who'd gotten me the job. My best friend Marrianne started a few months after me. I'd gotten her the job and we were both proud to call ourselves bakers. And Paula, a single mom in her mid-forties who wore Daisy Dukes, looked *great* in them, and knew it. She'd reminisce about her "hoochie days," as she called them. She had two teenage daughters, and when she found cigarettes or condoms in her daughters' jackets, she wasn't mad, she was proud. She'd cackle, "A chip off the old block!" laughing and smiling. We adored her.

I want to tell you about bread.

It starts with the mixer. The mixer makes the dough. I was never a mixer, so I honestly don't know much about it. Paula was the head mixer and was really good at it.

After the dough was mixed, it was put into round plastic containers the size of an outdoor trash bin. When the dough had risen enough, one of the stronger bakers would lift the bin up and pour the heavy mountain of dough onto the bread table. The one time I tried I nearly fell over and we all laughed.

The kneading table was large and wooden, the surface area of a queen-sized bed. The cutter stood at the end and used a metal scraper to cut hunks of dough from the big central mound. Each hunk was measured on a scale until it weighed the proper amount and then tossed to one of us for kneading and shaping. Being the cutter was fun. We rotated the job and maintained a friendly competition over who could get the weight of the dough exactly right on the first cut, but usually it was over or under and you had to add a tiny bit of dough or cut out a sliver from a too-heavy piece. When you got good at cutting, you went fast and it sounded really cool—the quick, decisive chop of the metal through dough on the wooden table, the springy squeak of the scale, and the soft, floury slap of the measured dough, classic rock on the radio.

Rich and Sher usually joined in on the action at the table. Rich especially loved to do it, and he was the one who taught me how to knead—fast and efficient, using the heel of your hand to turn, push, fold, repeat. I liked how the cold dough felt between my fingers, how soft it was against my floury forearms and elbows.

After kneading the dough, we shaped it. Some loaves, like cinnamon swirl and pumpkin bread, went into rectangular tins. Challah was braided, focaccia was spread and pressed with dappled fingers. But most of our loaves came in rounds and that's where the real shaping action happened. Using your forearms to spin and tuck, spin and tuck, spin and tuck till it was a firm dome with a taut top. It took strength and an experienced touch to get the top tension right—too loose and it became globbery and misshapen. Too taut and it would split on top. It required forearm strength, so it was difficult to shape a loaf if your elbows were lower than the table, which my short-ass self was, so Rich made me a raised platform to stand on.

Once the loaves were shaped, they were put on trays lined with parchment paper and scored with a small knife—pretty patterns sliced onto the taut tops, each kind of bread with its own specific design. Then the trays went into the oven. The oven was the size of a small bedroom with large shelves that rotated like a Ferris wheel. When the loaves were ready to go in, you pushed the sliding oven door up, a wave of heat coming at you, and pressed a button to stop the rotation of the shelves. I enjoyed pressing that button, trying to time it so that the shelf was exactly level with the ledge when it stopped. Then you slid in the trays of raw loaves and put a peg in a round timer and then wrote the peg and corresponding bread info on a dry erase board. Because there were often several different kinds of bread baking in the oven, we used colored pegs to indicate the baking time progress for each one. Or for the timing of other things: when to remove loaves from the proofer, when to add crushed pecans to the holiday bread, when to spray the sourdough.

If a batch of dough turned out bad—over- or under-proofed, etc.—you still had to bake it because if you threw it away as raw dough it might expand and overwhelm the dumpster. So we'd bake the dough-gone-bad in one huge mound before tossing it out. Sometimes we played around with it if we had time, shaping it into animals or letters that spelled our names. Once, when Rich and Sher weren't there, we made a bread version of Dirk Diggler from *Boogie Nights*, complete with his, um, diggler. It was so funny.

When the timer went off, the hot loaves were pulled out of the oven and placed on wire racks to cool. Once they were cool, we bagged them in clear plastic bags with a paper label tucked inside. You can't bag bread when it's warm because the steam will condense on the plastic and make the bread soggy—so if a customer bought a hot loaf, we tucked it in an open brown paper bag and handed them a plastic bag and a twist tie, instructing them to put it in the plastic bag once it was completely cool.

I was there for about three years, working my way up from the counter to the kneading table to head pastry chef. Because we were a bread bakery, being pastry chef wasn't as prestigious as it sounds—I didn't even mix the pastry dough—but that's what they called the position. We made a few simple pastries. Muffins, oatmeal cookies, cinnamon rolls. It was pretty easy. For the muffins I scooped batter into tins and made a crumb topping. The cookie dough was mixed by the mixer and I just scooped the dough into balls and placed them, three by four, on trays before shoving them into the oven. But the cinnamon rolls—*those* were my specialty.

The cinnamon roll dough was always premixed the prior evening so that it would be cold the next morning. I'd pull it out of the fridge and dump the huge mound of dough onto the bread table. It's a thicker dough, the consistency some-where between regular bread dough and Play-Doh. Using my hands first, then a rolling pin, I spread it out till it cov-ered half the table, length-wise—about the size of a yoga mat. Then I spread two bricks of softened butter all over the dough, like a kid finger painting. The butter, creamy and cold, was so good on my hands in a way that felt clean. After evenly spreading the butter, I scooped cinnamon sugar out of a bin with a large tin shovel and poured it all over the but-ter. Then came the rolling. Starting at the longways edge of the flattened dough yoga mat, I rolled the whole thing into a snake shape.

I was proud of my dough-rolling technique. I made the beginning of the rolls (the inner part) looser, and gradually tightened the roll as I got to the outer edge. This was important, because if the center was rolled too tight, it would pop out and spill over in the oven. (Which Paula called "erection rolls," haha.) But if you rolled it too loose it sank in the middle. My rolls always had a perfectly uniform rise. Once I'd rolled the whole thing into a long six-foot cinnamon dough snake, I cut it in two-inch slices (our cinnamon rolls were big), which held their round shape because the dough was still cold from the refrigerator. I liked the way the knife cut the dough so cleanly, the color of the dark brown swirls in white dough. I laid them out flat in circles, eight to a tray. Half the batch was topped with crushed pecans—or was it walnuts? Then I slid the trays into the oven and put a peg in the timer.

When they came out of the oven, the dough was airy and light, the cinnamon mix fragrant and not too sweet. The consistency was way better than the gross, gummy, overly sweet buns you got at the mall. Those always made me feel sick. But at Montana Gold, when you broke open our cinnamon rolls, steam rose up out of them, and they weren't all sticky. Eating them felt almost wholesome.

Pastry and mixer opened the bakery. When I worked pastry, I'd wake up at 5:00 a.m. to drive the dark, empty suburban streets to the bakery. For the first few hours, it was just two people: me on pastry and Paula or Rich mixing. I loved the quiet of those early mornings, baking bread before the sun came up. It made me feel important, useful. As if the town were dormant and we ran the machinery that made the day begin. The bread-kneading team would arrive later, at 7:00 a.m. Then the bakery would open for business at 8:30 a.m., just as the first steaming loaves were being pulled out of the oven.

Holiday time at Montana Gold was special. The bakery would be busier than usual. We made seasonal loaves like gingerbread in disposable aluminum tins, or "holiday bread," which was a much more delicious version of a fruitcake. Though we always had regulars at the bakery, new people came in during the holiday season. It was a pleasure to introduce them to our bread. They would buy fresh dinner rolls to bring to a holiday party or cinnamon swirl bread to make their kids French toast on Christmas morning. The bustle of the holidays was wonderful. It made us all feel a sense of purpose. We were making people's bread and we would make it the best bread they ever had. In wintertime, it got dark earlier, around 4:00 p.m., and when I worked the closing shifts, it was exciting to approach the bakery in the dark—the fluorescent lights of the spare white bakery glowed from the inside as if to say *We are open. We are working.* I was proud to be a part of that team. I only made $5.25 an hour, minimum wage in Virginia back then. After a year they gave me a raise of $0.50 an hour, which was kind of laughable, but I didn't care. I liked it there.

One day, a rival bakery opened up. It was called Good Grain and it was very different from Montana Gold. Good Grain didn't mill their own flour; they had it delivered in bulk. Their decor was colorful—the whole bakery painted in reds and yellows and purples. There was a mural of a sunrise on the wall. Streamers and sparkly decorations hung from the ceiling in accordance with the holidays. They even had a play area with toys for kids.

Marrianne was always the more financially ambitious of the two of us, so when Good Grain offered her more money, she defected. I wanted to remain loyal to Rich and Sher, but eventually Marrianne convinced me to defect because Good Grain paid ten dollars an hour. I told Rich I was quitting, but I felt too guilty to tell him the real reason why. . . . "I got a job at the Gap, so I could get discounts on clothes!" I explained, my face burning. I told myself it wasn't a lie because it was half-true—I *had* gotten a part-time summer job at the Gap but I only worked there two shifts a week to get the discount . . . and only ended up staying one month (folding clothes was so boring). I'm pretty sure Rich knew that I went to the new bakery with Marrianne (Marrianne had been honest when she quit), but he never pressed me. He just hugged me and thanked me and wished me well. "We'll miss you," he said. I smiled and hurried out as fast as I could, trying to outrun my guilt.

Good Grain was actually a franchise that masqueraded as a family business, and I guess in some ways it was. It was operated by a religious married couple named Norm and Sally. They were very chipper in a way Marrianne and I mistrusted. I'm naturally a little cynical and Marrianne is *really* cynical, and to us, their cheery positivity had the stink of targeted judgment. Norm was bald and fat with bright blue eyes that were a weird combination of bewildered and smug. Sally was snobby and self-satisfied. She carried designer bags and always had a perfect manicure. Not once did she knead the dough at the bread table like Sher did. They had a bunch of kids who were spoiled brats and Sally treated them like little gods. One time, one of the kids blasted Marrianne in the face with a Super Soaker water gun that was filled with moldy water. It got all over the kneading table. I scolded the kid—"NO! You are not allowed to do that!" And then Sally scolded me for scolding her kid. She grabbed the kid, petting him and taking him out of the kitchen. She didn't speak to me for a few days.

My job was safe, though, because Marrianne and I were essential to that place. Sally wasn't a baker. She was there to decorate and gossip with all the suburban moms who came in. Norm wasn't a great baker either; he was reading from the franchise manual. He didn't even know why you couldn't throw raw dough into the dumpster! Marrianne and I rolled our eyes in disbelief. We had to *teach* him. Eventually, Norm even handed the mixing duties over to Marrianne. Which is insane . . . to have a teenager be the mixer? The most important job in the bakery? Looking back, it was obvious that they didn't care or understand what it meant to make bread. At one point, Good Grain started selling ice cream. *What even* is *this place?* I wondered, bakery purist to the end.

Nevertheless, Good Grain was in a trendier shopping center and was newer and cooler. Sally was fashionable, and all the local moms came in to chat and gossip with her. It became a hot spot. Before I left Montana Gold, I know that Rich and Sher saw their sales go down. But I never heard them say a bad word about Good Grain. Though you could feel their worry, they were quiet about it.

But at Good Grain, Norm constantly insulted Rich and Sher. Especially Rich. One time, when we needed to bake off some overproofed dough, he shaped it into a body, baked it, hung it from the ceiling, and named it Rich. And then he threw stuff at it, laughing, encouraging everyone else to mock it too. It was really mean and unnecessary. Rich had never said or done anything bad to Norm.

Norm also played favorites, which Marrianne and I *hated* because we were *not* the favorites, even though we were the best bakers on their very immature staff. A teenage girl from the local private school (Marrianne and I went to public school) was the favorite. We were pissed because we had no doubt she was only hired because her parents were family friends of Norm and Sally's. We were also pissed because rumor had it that she was paid more than everyone else. Her name was Jane and she wasn't even a good baker. She didn't even know how to shape dinner rolls! (There's a certain technique you have to do with your hands to make dinner rolls; it's tricky to get the hang of, to knead and shape the rolls with a taut top with just the palm of your hand and curled fingers. It's hard to describe and even harder to teach. It's one of those things that you keep doing, and one day you just, like, *get* it.) Eventually Norm bought a machine that automatically made the dinner rolls. Marrianne and I were insulted. A machine to make dinner rolls? We made dinner rolls *by hand*. But not at Good Grain. They catered to their worst baker instead of teaching her how to get better at it. Rich and Sher had taught us how to be real bakers.

A few months after Marrianne and I went away to college, Good Grain shuttered unexpectedly. We were surprised because as far as we knew business had been booming there. So Marrianne did a little digging, privately asking another former Good Grain employee what happened. He told her that he heard Good Grain shut down not because of poor business or bad bread but because of scandal!! The rumors were that middle-aged Norm and teenage Jane were caught kissing in the back of the bakery, Norm and Sally divorced, Jane's parents cut them off, and Norm left town. Neither of us ever heard from him again. True or not, Marrianne and I still talk about it today because of how, even as teenagers, we'd always thought Norm's religious moral superiority felt a little phony. And also? Because when we pictured the two of them hooking up it made us want to barf. Like . . . omg ew ewww GROSS.

With Good Grain gone, Montana Gold was once again *the* bread bakery in town. When low-carb diets became fashionable around the early 2000s, they closed the Parham Road location I'd primarily worked at. But their Carytown bakery stayed in business. When I was home from college for a couple of Christmas breaks, Rich and Sher let me work the holiday-rush weeks to make some extra money. They never mentioned my betrayal at Good Grain; they were just glad I came back.

When I moved to New York City after college, I stopped going home to Richmond very often and lost my connection with Montana Gold. But I still think of Rich and Sher with fondness. They taught me what it means to bake bread. I wonder what their lives are like now. Do they have grandkids? Does Rich still have his mustache? Does Mrs. Peskin still come in on focaccia day? Sometimes, when I'm back in town, I drive by, and I'm tempted to stop in, but I get shy. For some reason, I think I'd feel embarrassed to see Rich and Sher. Embarrassed of having grown up. My acting career feels flimsy next to something as substantial and real as a loaf of bread. Or maybe I'm scared that they won't remember me, when they meant so much to me. I hope they know how much they gave me when they taught me about making bread.

When Good Grain opened, it was cool and buzzy and paid lots more money. It had bright colors! It had gloss and flair! Montana Gold was spare and simple and made good bread and made your hair white when you walked out of the mill room. But it's the one that lasted, that is still standing. It remains, to this day, my favorite job I ever had.

Holding my little sister

Snap and Whistle

I have three sisters. My two older sisters are a year apart. Then there was a big gap before I came along. The youngest, E, was born almost exactly two years later. My little sister. Because of the age difference, the four of us girls naturally split into pairs—the older two and the younger two. The older sisters fought a lot, but E and I were close. As little kids, we had double birthday parties together, shared a room, and wore the same underwear. She was able to snap her fingers and I couldn't snap my fingers, and I was able to whistle, and she couldn't whistle, and we concluded that that meant we completed each other—one could snap; the other could whistle.

After dinner, I'd go, "E, want to play with Bees?" which was our "code" for Barbies, and she'd nod happily and we'd head upstairs to our room. We liked walking up the stairs on all fours, slapping each step with our hands as we climbed. Our parents wouldn't buy us a Barbie house, so we made one with Kleenex boxes and blankets under the corner desk of our room. We each had one Barbie and they shared a Ken. In all my memories of childhood playtime, E is there beside me:

braiding our Barbies' hair, stringing together bead necklaces, working on jigsaw puzzles, hula-hooping in the driveway. We took the same gymnastics classes, played with the same kids, went to our neighbor's pool together. Our room had twin beds next to each other, and as we were falling asleep, we'd play a game where one of us would tap out a rhythm on our mattress and the other had to guess the song.

Dad was a biology and genetics professor at Virginia Commonwealth University. In the summertime, E and I sometimes went to work with him. We loved hanging out in his office. It had big wicker sofas and cupboards filled with things like Nescafé, sugar cubes, apple cinnamon tea bags, and Cup O' Noodles. There was an electric kettle, a dry-erase board that we constantly drew on, and a xerox machine where we'd copy dollar bills or our hands. There were two boxy gray IBM computers, and Dad let us use one of them to play King's Quest on CD-ROM. Dad loved plants, so there were plants everywhere, including a tree that had been little when he first moved in but had grown enormous, its branches pushing against the high ceiling. We'd stare up at its canopy of leaves and wonder how he would ever get it out.

Dad liked having us there. He kept a jar of coins near the door of his office that we pilfered to buy chips or Juicy Fruit gum from the vending machine down the hall. That was probably half the reason we liked going to work with him: we knew we'd get vending machine treats. He kept pictures of us on his desk in wooden frames that we'd decorated with puffy paint and glitter as a Christmas present one year. I stared at mine a lot because I liked how I looked in it, hair parted on the side, wearing my silk magenta blouse that I was so proud of (the beginning signs of my budding vanity).

His office was connected to his lab next door, where E and I were allowed to wander in and out, unsupervised. We weren't the kind of kids who broke things. We walked around freely, talking to his lab assistants or just looking at the neat science-y things: petri dishes of agar, workstations with sliding glass doors and ventilation hoods, a water distiller, and filled beakers on trays that moved round and round to keep the fluids continuously mobile. E and I stared at those trays a lot, mesmerized by the swirling liquids.

One summer, we went through a POG phase. Nineties kids will remember POGs. Dad drove us to the craft store after work to buy all the POGs we wanted. He was happy to get them because they were only around ten cents each. We kept them in a pink plastic sleeve the size of a toilet paper roll with our two sparkly slammers on top. We brought them to the lab every day to play POGs on the floor with his assistants. The lab assistants were grad students, in their twenties. They were all nice to us. One of the lab assistants sometimes brought his acoustic guitar. We liked listening to him play and I had a big crush on him. I constantly giggled at everything he said, even when he wasn't trying to be funny.

If we wanted to read or watch videos, the university library was right next door to Dad's building. He'd give us his faculty card and let us go over there by ourselves, where we read the comics and Dear Abby or Ann Landers from daily newspapers secured to wooden dowels. Or we'd check out VHS cassettes and headphones, watching them in the library's mini-TV viewing cubbies. My favorite videos were the PBS special concerts. The library had microfiche too, which we thought was so neat. I guess, now that we have the internet, microfiche probably doesn't exist anymore.

Compared to the parenting styles I see today, it's amazing to think how free our parents let us be: walking across a college campus alone, wandering in and out of a science lab unsupervised. We were free at home too. Mom never monitored our schoolwork, and she let us play outside every day. We never needed to tell her what we were doing or where we were going so long as we were back home in time for dinner. For hours a day we roamed the neighborhood or the woods by ourselves, and she never knew or worried about our whereabouts.

Sometimes we went to Jessie McKenzie's house down the street, knocking on her door and asking her mom if Jessie could come out and play. Jessie had a big golden retriever that E and I both loved. Then the three of us kids stomped through the woods, leash-less dog behind us, to a little creek where we caught tadpoles and skipped stones. We gathered long branches and draped them against a tree to make a fort. Jessie's dog watched over us, wagging her tail.

E and I loved dogs, but we never had one growing up. So if Jessie wasn't home, we'd knock on random doors in the neighborhood and say, "Hi. Do you have a dog? Can we walk your dog?" Even though lots of people had no idea who we were (because we would venture FAR from our house), we were little kids so they always said yes. Many of them seemed amused as they handed over the leash with a smile. That was the neighborhood we grew up in—trusting, friendly. We loved walking the different dogs around the neighborhood, taking turns holding the leash, petting and cooing and squealing. One of the dogs was named Samantha, a small black poodle with a gentle disposition. We loved her because she knew how to *sit* and *shake*. Sometimes she had bows in her hair!

We lived in a deep woodsy part of a subdivision, so there wasn't any traffic. You could be out there for an entire day without seeing a single car go by, so it was safe for us to ride our bikes. There was a steep dip between two hills in the road near our house, and we loved to ride down it, trying not to chicken out when the bikes went really fast. You *wanted* them to go fast so the momentum made the uphill on the other side easier. My bike was pastel purple with a banana seat that had a rainbow on it. I knew how to *stand* on top of my moving bike. Well, sort of—it was this trick I did where I put my feet on the seat of the bike and straightened my legs up, so I was "standing" on the seat, but my torso was still bent over, hands clutching the handlebars. I'd just cruise like that: butt in the air, torso hunched over as I held the handlebars, so very casual, thinking I looked impressive. But I probably looked like an orangutan on wheels.

E and I both did gymnastics, and we found a fallen tree

trunk deep in the woods that we used as a balance beam . . . doing back walkovers, full turns, and handstands. We made up entire routines, finishing them with barani dismounts. We copied the styles of the Olympic gymnasts we loved—Kim Zmeskal and Shannon Miller and Dominique Dawes—including their finishing finger positions. Shannon Miller splayed her hands like a fan, which is how I did mine. Kim Zmeskal had the more traditional middle finger down toward the thumb, and that was E's move.

If we fell off the tree trunk, the landing was soft—it was only about twelve inches from a ground padded with leaves. In my memories of that time, everything was soft—the damp tree bark and dusky sunsets. The fall leaves so abundant it felt like we waded in them, rather than walked. Coming home from the bus stop, E and I enjoyed kicking them up from the ground or catching them in the air as they fell. We kept track of how many leaves we caught, comparing the numbers from the previous day. The walk from the bus stop was long, so we invented lots of games along the way. Like trying to get home by only stepping on crunchy leaves (anything else was lava!). Or taking turns kicking a pebble all the way from the bus stop to home, acting mock scared when the pebble almost went "out of bounds" (off the road and onto a neighbor's lawn). E was snap and I was whistle and we were best friends.

When I went to middle school, our buses were on different schedules. Suddenly, I was the only kid at that bus stop. I tried to chase the falling leaves myself or kick a pebble all the way home, but it wasn't as fun without E. I imagine kids today would look at their phones on long walks home, but cell phones didn't exist then, so I had to come up with new games to play without E. My best one was racing the mailman. He was often in his mail car near my bus stop when I got off, and I'd RACE him to my house. Which is hilarious in hindsight. It became a kind of silent understanding between us to the point where he started waiting for me. I'd jump out of the bus and spot him, and he'd wave *GO!* I'd sprint home with all my might, backpack bouncing up and down, trying to beat a dude in a car. Having a car may have seemed an advantage, *except* for the fact that he had to stop at mailboxes along the way. That's how I thought I could beat him, and you know what? I always did! The houses were spaced far apart, though, so I had to sprint pretty hard between mailboxes. When I finally got home, I'd be panting, out of breath, waiting for him by our mailbox (the "finish line"). He was a nice, older Black gentleman and I'm pretty sure he drove slower to let me win. "You beat me!" he'd say as he handed me our mail. I'd nod, serious, as a way of apologizing for destroying him with my incredible speed. There was one point where I honestly thought maybe I could become an Olympic runner one day because I was able to beat a guy *in a car*.

Olympic dreams aside, I missed my little sister, but I wasn't sure she missed me. Whereas I was bold and daring, she was always the gentle and quiet one—the introvert to my extrovert, the snap to my whistle. Maybe she liked not having me around, I worried. Maybe that meant she could finally shine. As little kids, we'd liked how our differences complemented each other. But as I grew up and started worrying about perception, I began questioning which was the "better" way to be. I started thinking her way was better, more likable. A lot of the books I loved romanticized introverts. The Southern culture we grew up in seemed to praise sweetness in girls more than boldness. "Little girls should be seen and not heard," people would say.

An early moment of this awareness happened at the dentist's office. E and I both had checkups—her appointment took a little longer than mine, so when I was done, I was sent back to the waiting room to sit with my mom. When E came out, two female dental assistants were guiding her. They were smitten—fawning over her, praising her quietness. She was clutching three toys she had gotten out of the treasure chest. We always got a toy from the treasure chest at the dentist's office. But they'd forgotten to offer me one that day. And E had gotten *extra* toys. I looked at her sweet, quiet face as she clutched the three toys and felt my eyes prickle. It was one of the first times I remember trying not to cry. *They didn't open the treasure chest for me because they don't like me*, I thought. *They like her better.* If I cried, I'd draw attention to that fact, and I didn't want anyone to know, because I was embarrassed that the two pretty dental assistants maybe didn't like me. That they liked her better. I didn't play Barbies with E that night.

E started making her own friends right around the time I was having difficulties with my own middle school friend group. I was too ashamed to tell anyone and I started becoming jealous of her. We used to be a pair, but now she had her own friends. As E started to find herself, she began to drift away from me.

It sparked a kind of terror inside and I began acting out against E. I was a teenager by then, and my feelings were enormous. I forbade her from borrowing my clothes, and when she tried to sneak them out of the closet, I yelled at her. I made stupid, mean rules for her, like saying she could only hang out with her friend Lexi if Lexi didn't call the house for one whole week. One time, I slapped her in the face during an argument over what TV show to watch. To this day, I'm still ashamed of that. I can't believe I hit my little sister.

And then we kind of became strangers. I was mean and controlling and she shut herself off from me as a way of protecting herself. I overcompensated with snobbery and distance, trying to pretend the hurt away. The only place I felt safe and happy was in community theater, where extroverts were celebrated. I began spending all my time doing plays or in acting classes. E began an obsession with AOL chat rooms, spending hours at a time in front of the computer. The family dynamic was shifting, too. Our two older sisters were adults and had moved out of the house long ago and our parents had started sleeping in separate rooms.

Then I left for college—going to New York for theater school. Two weeks later, our parents separated. E chose to live with our dad for her remaining two years of high school. That must have been a hard time for her, choosing who to live with, alone at home amid all that drama. But she never talked about it, and I never asked. I started dating a thirty-year-old guy and spent all my time and energy on him—thinking that if I got him to love me, that would somehow prove something.

Between high school and our mid-thirties E and I only shared one moment of real closeness. I was a sophomore in college and she called me with questions about birth control. She was about to go on spring break with her boyfriend (I didn't even know she had a boyfriend!) and thought it might happen. She seemed nervous about asking me, but I was so glad she called me! It was nice to be the big sister again; nice to be helpful. I tried to make the conversation as safe, nonjudgmental, and easy as possible. Matter-of-fact in a way that took away any embarrassment. I told her about how I'd secretly been on birth control since high school (she had no idea!), how I'd gone to Planned Parenthood downtown on Monument Avenue, where you could get the pill and free condoms. I'd gone with my friend Annie and had hidden my pills in the pocket of a purse in the bottom of a box of clothes in the back of my closet. If E wanted to go on the pill, I reassured her that Planned Parenthood kept it private—

Mom and Dad wouldn't find out. I felt happy after that phone call. It was nice to feel close to her again.

But other than that, she was always distant and shut off around me. I don't blame her; I'd been awful to her in high school.

When I was in my early twenties and going through a bunch of therapy, I wrote her a long apology letter. Acknowledging how mean I'd been, saying that I was sorry. That I missed our friendship, but I understood her wariness. That she was a great person, and I was proud of her and supportive of anything she wanted to do. That I loved her. I repeated how sorry I was.

She never mentioned the letter, though I know she got it. I guess it would have been embarrassing for us both to talk about something like that. Especially for her. Sometimes it's hard to know if an apology is meant for the receiver's benefit or for the apologizer's own selfish gratification. Probably the latter. It was unkind of me to force a conversation that I knew she wasn't comfortable having.

Once, when she was up North touring a school in New Jersey, E came to meet me in the city so I could drive us both back down to Virginia for Thanksgiving. She was quiet and guarded, the way you understandably would be around someone who has hurt you. We were on the New Jersey Turnpike when the tire on my car blew out. I acted very dramatic. "OH MY GOD, this is my greatest fear! Breaking down on the Jersey Turnpike!" My dramatics made her giggle, so I really ramped it up. I wanted her to laugh and be less scared of me. I'd rather feel like a clown than a monster. We called AAA, got our tire patched, and continued down I-95. She was a little more relaxed; I was a little more hopeful.

It was only a temporary reprieve. As she got older and more confident, she'd sort of jab me when we were home for the holidays with our boyfriends. At the dinner table she'd poke fun at me by telling all the stories of how mean I'd been to her as a teenager. She and her boyfriend would laugh and give each other knowing glances as if they had discussed me before. I usually became glib or quiet. Glib worked best—I could hide my hurt. I already felt guilty and regretful; better to let her have a little joke. To pretend it didn't bother me.

But she brought it up often, and only when we were around other people. She was always casual about it, so I tried to be casual too. Until one day, when I was in my late twenties, home for the holidays. We were in her car, me in the backseat, she and her new boyfriend up front. She was cracking snide jokes about how crazy mean I used to be, how I forbade her from hanging out with specific friends and screamed at her for trying to wear my clothes. I became quiet in the backseat, in a way that I knew revealed my guilt. She was driving, her boyfriend gazing at her adoringly as he stroked her hair—I could tell that he already knew the stories. That she was the innocent victim and I was the evil villain in his imagined picture of our childhoods. But he'd only just met me. He didn't know anything.

Suddenly, out of nowhere, I broke down crying. Loud, heaving sobs punctuated by gasps of despair.

It scared them both at first. The power of my emotions can do that sometimes, which is why I've always tried to suppress them. I want to be calm and introverted like her. To have the dental assistants like me too. But I couldn't hold it in anymore. Between sobs, I choked out everything I'd held back over the years: How she was right. How I was ashamed of myself and hated myself for it. How I *knew* she had gotten the apology letter I sent her years ago. How she *knew* I had been trying to be better. I had been kind and supportive and deferential to her for the past decade. Didn't those years of good behavior count for anything? Would I never be allowed to amend the mistakes I made as a kid? It was like she *wanted* me to remain the mean, sad teenager. Couldn't I be allowed to change, the way I had let her change? Weeping, I said all I wanted was to be friends again, and I knew that wasn't gonna happen but could she at least please stop shaming me for something I was already ashamed of?

Yes. I was a damn adult, and I sobbed all that shit. I'm a fucking sobber. I hate it and I've tried to squelch it, but sometimes I just can't.

E was quiet. Her boyfriend, not used to the intensity of my emotions the way she was, tried to calm me down. They both wanted me to stop crying. He wanted me to stop because it made him uncomfortable. But she wanted me to stop because she's my sister and she loves me—the mean me, the clown me, the crying me, the me who snapped and whistled with her. And she didn't want me to be sad. I think she finally saw that I hurt as much as she had all those years ago. We were even, I guess. Or maybe she realized that we weren't in a battle; we were on the same side, even if we were far apart.

She never mentioned my childhood mean stuff after that.

It's funny, I was so confident when we were little kids. But she is the more secure one now. She's still an introvert, and I'm still very extro, but she seems to have a quiet, grounded sense of her self-worth, whereas I constantly question my own. My identity has always felt like it's in perpetual flux, except when I'm acting and I'm *assigned* a role.

She still has a subtle wariness around me. I've accepted that, because I know I earned it and because I know that I'm a lot to handle. Back when we were kids, I was so scared of losing her as my best friend. I did lose her in that role, but she's still my sister. She'll always be my sister. And I'm not scared of losing her anymore, because I realize she was never mine to begin with. Her life is her own. She should have an inner life and friendships that I am not a part of, and will never be a part of, the way I now have those things for myself too. I guess that's what growing up is.

When I shared this essay with her to get her permission to publish it, I wasn't worried. I know my sister. She texted me after a few days:

I think the one thing you're missing from your essay is how I was very much your follower. You would test the boundaries of something, and make it feel safer for me to maybe try. You were the fearless one, the person who protected me from [the neighborhood bully] and his mean taunts. The one who always had a point of reference for other people sucking and could see outside other people's lame values.

I've always admired your strength, drive, and how bold you are in everything you do. But yeah, I did feel very much rejected by you in middle school. It's surprising to hear that you missed me too.

Too.

Btw I don't remember wearing the same underwear. That's kinda gross lol.

Omg I meant like after it was washed. CLEAN, it was the same clean underwear haha

In 1996, there was a blizzard in Virginia. It wasn't one of those windy blizzards; it was calm. The still air filled with slow, fat snowflakes that floated down like feathers. School was canceled for two whole weeks, and E and I sometimes snuck out late at night to sit against the garage door and look up at the sky. The motion-sensor floodlights would come on, and we could watch the snowflakes fall from the darkness through the beams of light. We both knew it was magic, so we didn't need to say anything. We just sat next to each other in the quiet watching the snow fall. After a while the floodlights would turn off, and one of us would jog out ten feet to trigger the motion sensor so the light would come back on. We did that for a long time. Just watching the snow above us, falling through the light. When we were done, we padded back inside and went to sleep.

Sisters

With Molly in New Orleans, 2009

Impeach the President

When I was in eighth grade, I hated a girl so much that I wanted to cut off all her hair.

We'd been best friends first, of course. At the beginning of sixth grade, Fiona was new in town, having moved to Richmond from Long Island, New York. We met on the school bus. She was wearing a *Les Misérables* sweatshirt, so I said hi. After discovering our mutual love for Broadway musicals and Converse One Star sneakers, we became instant friends. She introduced me to hamantaschen, Mason Pearson hairbrushes, and Betsey Johnson dresses, which I coveted but couldn't afford. She had a cute pet hamster. She lived in a huge, modernist house with a pool and actual art inside, including a sculpture encircled by a massive spiral staircase in their high-ceilinged foyer. Her bedroom had its own bathroom—I'd never heard of a kid having such a luxury! She was pretty and sophisticated and from *New York*, and I was very impressed by her.

At the end of seventh grade, she ran for vice president against Becca Watson, the most popular girl in school. Becca was a friendly, blond cheerleader with good grades, so I knew the election would be a challenge for Fiona. I became her "campaign manager" and I took my job seriously. Just like in a real election, there were caps on how much you could spend for promotion and what you could do. For example, you were allowed to make posters and stickers, but you weren't allowed to give out cookies or treats, because that was considered a bribe. Most candidates made only posters and stickers with slogans like "A vote for Jim is a vote to win." But stickers were boring, so my marketing strategy was different. Fiona played infield for the softball team, and the movie *Angels in the Outfield* had come out a couple years earlier. Our slogan? "Vote for Fiona, the Angel in the *In*field!"

The "angel" was part of my campaign strategy. I knew what girls liked: accessories. So I bought a bunch of glittery gold pipe cleaners and twisted two together in a circle to form a halo. Then I attached a small ribbon on the back that said, "Fiona for VP." If you wore a halo, you were voting for Fiona. I made like fifty of them every day after school, and handed them out by the buses every morning. They were a hit. The girls loved them and even the boys would wear them to get laughs. It was cooler than a sticker; people who didn't even know Fiona wore them.

Each candidate had to give a speech in front of the whole grade. The speech Fiona wrote was standard. *We should have better options in the cafeteria. More soda machines. More spirit days.* But her speech was kinda boring, so I rewrote it and made it funny in a way that suited her. And

against all odds, against the most popular girl in school . . .
she won! I was so happy. It felt good to help my best friend.

The summer before eighth grade, we had a different
goal. Boys! She had a crush on Alex Bloomfield—a smart,
wholesome kid with blond hair and brown eyes—and I had
a crush on Ben Jones, a skinny boy who wore band T-shirts.
Before the school year started, Fiona and I made a pact to
call our crushes on the phone. Nervous, we planned it all
out—how to open the call (casual), what to say (light, easy
fare); we even made a list of emergency topics/stories that
we could talk about in case there was an awkward silence.
We each went home with Mission-Call-a-Boy, promising to
report back the next day. Clutching the emergency topics
list in my hand, I locked myself in my room, sat on the floor
with the tan phone and the pale blue middle school directory, and dialed.

"Hi. Is Ben there?"

I didn't end up needing the list. Ben and I had a great
conversation where everything just flowed. Before we knew
it, we had been talking on the phone for an hour. Ever since
that call, I've always enjoyed phone calls over texts. Texts feel
catered to social handicaps . . . like those lists of topics that
Fiona and I had written. They are vetted and preplanned . . .
at least a little. You can't hear reactions in real time. There's
no in-the-moment wit, no voices with pauses or natural
turn-taking. You don't ever get to hear laughter. "LOL" will
never beat the sound of real human laughter. And without

that, there's no . . . magic. How do you find intimacy without magic?

But maybe that's just me. Because Fiona's phone call did not go so well. She'd had to consult her list and was nervous the whole time. Whereas Ben and I continued talking on the phone every day, I could tell Fiona felt bad. So I suggested a group date—that we all go to Kings Dominion, the local theme park, together.

We were old enough that our parents could drop us off at the park and pick us up at a designated time. It was Fiona, Ben, Alex, and me. We also included the redheaded class-clown kid named Peter so it didn't feel like a weird double date. We rode roller coasters, ate funnel cake, drank red- or blue-colored drinks, and felt like cool teenagers because we were without adult supervision. After that, the five of us became a solid friend group. We had our designated table at lunch and went to the mall together. Along the way, we adopted a girl named Sarah into our group and the guy she had a crush on, Cory. We were all in the school's Drama Club, and we were typical theater kids—extroverted, entertaining, unafraid. People had fun around us, and we became popular in a way that the jocks and cheerleaders couldn't touch. Fiona and I were the leaders of the group.

Ben and I were still tight, talking on the phone after school every day. I talked to other boys on the phone too. But try as she might, Fiona failed to connect romantically with Alex. Even though she was really pretty, Fiona wasn't great at talking to boys one-on-one yet. Whereas she and I used to giggle about crushes, now we barely talked about them. Either oblivious or cruel or both, I'd brag about all the boys who called me, rolling my eyes with a carefree smile.

One morning, she turned on me. We were on the school bus when I made a careless comment about a zit she had, and she flipped out. I don't know what she said or how she managed to do it, but in one day, she turned our whole friend group against me. Even Ben. It was a total coup.

I was so confused. For days I cried, apologized, begged her forgiveness. But she gave me the silent treatment. She wouldn't make eye contact and walked away while I was apologizing. Or she'd turn to Sarah and say, "Did you hear anything just now? I didn't. Maybe it was the wind." It was my first experience with the silent treatment, and it hurt. Rather than an argument or blatant insults, her silence rendered me invisible.

The whole friend group followed Fiona's lead. It actually fortified them, having me as a common enemy. I'd enter the lunchroom to their jeers and boos and have to sit alone. Sometimes they even threw stuff at me—napkins or straws or spitballs. I tried to hold my head high, focusing on other things that mattered to me, like the Drama Club. Earlier that year I had been elected president of the club. I was proud of my title and responsibilities. One of my ideas was a suggestion box. I took a shoebox, carefully covered it in a sparkly gift wrap, wrote the words "Drama Club Suggestions" in glittery puffy paint, and placed it on the windowsill. At our weekly Drama Club meetings, I would read aloud all of the suggestions in the box—what plays we should look at, improv exercises, commentary, etc.

After Fiona turned the group against me, they stuffed the suggestion box with notes that said "The president sucks" and "Impeach the president" and "The president has a mustache" (which particularly stung, because Fiona did too! She was the one who'd taught me to use Sally Hansen cream hair bleach to lighten my upper lip hair!). It was as dramatic as you could imagine. There I was, at our weekly meeting, standing in front of everybody, preparing to read from the suggestion box. When I pulled out the first few slips of paper, my heart contracted, and I couldn't even speak. I left the room crying. When Mr. Frizzell, the drama teacher, came out to ask me what was wrong, I heard their laughter back inside the classroom. No one was punished because the suggestion box was anonymous. I wouldn't have wanted them to be punished anyway; that would have just drawn more attention to the fact that they didn't like me anymore.

So anyway. That's why I wanted to cut off all of Fiona's hair.

Even though it's petty and dumb, I'm almost proud of that revenge fantasy. Proud that the *most* painful, *nastiest* thing I could think of was for her to have, like, the WORST hair. As far as revenge goes, it's pretty tame.

This story is not that unusual or especially traumatic. Everyone gets bullied or hurt in some way during their childhood. Kids can be cruel. It's a normal part of life. Childhood is a testing ground for what type of person you want to be, and part of that is trying things out, including cruelty, and seeing how it feels. Does it make you feel better? Or worse? Powerful? Or full of regret?

The first few days after they banished me from their lunch table, I sat alone and was ashamed. But one day, a girl named Molly invited me to sit with her and her friends.

Molly was neither popular nor unpopular. She had a quiet, dry wit. She had an old dog with a tumor and a graying snout and there were pictures of Brad Pitt and Gwyneth Paltrow all over her bedroom walls. She even looked kind of like Gwyneth Paltrow. I sat with her at lunch that day, grateful for the invitation, and we became friends. We both liked art and photography. We both thought the paintings of Thomas Kinkade were, like, *extraordinary*, which is both embarrassing and adorable (oh God, I miss the days before snobbery). We obsessed over boys we liked, sometimes even pretending to create witch spells to get them to fall in love with us. Over the summers, she lived with her dad in western Massachusetts, and we became pen pals, sending letters to each other in the mail. For fun, we would stuff the envelopes with random things—Crystal Light packets, ultra-thin maxi pads, or perfume samples ripped out of magazines.

When I confessed my horrible hair cutting revenge fantasy to Molly, I was terrified she'd think I was crazy. But . . . she didn't judge me; she laughed! What a relief it was to share something bad about myself and still be loved! Her laugh took the shame out of it. And instead of being an itch I needed to scratch, it became a joke between us. The confession and laughter felt better than executing the actual fantasy.

Fiona never let up on the silent treatment. During our junior and senior years of high school, she and I were in the same chorus class—the most selective one in our school, the ten-girl a cappella chorus called the Downbeats. Despite being in such a small, intimate singing group, she still refused to speak to me or even make eye contact. Junior year of the Downbeats, I tried kissing up to her. I complimented her often, smiling as brightly as I could, hoping to connect. But it didn't work. After a while, I just accepted her silence. When I was voted president of the Downbeats during our senior year, I figured a good leader would try to make things right, so I wrote her a letter apologizing for the awkward years, expressing gratitude for her talent in the chorus, and asking her if we could let it be water under the bridge—so we could move forward and have a great senior-year chorus experience together. I handed it to her and watched as she read it quietly. Then, without looking at me, she said, "Thanks, I appreciate that." And though her hostility toward me waned, she remained cold. I didn't see her again until years later, post-college, when we were both at an open casting call in New York for the national tour of *Rent*. I approached her and said hi. She barely acknowledged me. Her eyes darting around the room for an escape, she nodded *hey* and quickly walked away. Neither of us got a part in the show.

I don't hold on to any negative feelings about Fiona.

She's not a bad person. And I know I was insensitive about her acne and her struggle with boys. We were both just teenagers figuring things out. Even though it was hard having my friend group ostracize me, I'm grateful it happened, because that's how I met Molly.

Molly and I are still good friends. We both lived in New York in our twenties, which is a very *specific* experience. We've traveled together—to Florida for poolside margaritas, New Orleans for Jazz Fest, Park City for Sundance, Brighton Beach for Russian burlesque. We've celebrated and mourned many boyfriends. She knows about *all* of mine. All their dick sizes too (sorry, guyyyys). It's been twenty-seven years since Molly invited me to sit with her at lunch. We're both moms now with daughters of our own. "How can parents possibly handle more than one?" I asked her over the phone recently. "Day care and neglect!" she joked as we both laughed. "I heard that it's good to let your kids play with knives!" I added. "Day care and neglect and knives! Huzzah!" Though we were joking, I was half-serious. I know that kids eventually figure themselves out.

At Maybeury Elementary School

Of Course She Did

Though I'm passionate about acting and theater, that was my second love. My first love was books. Gosh, I *loved* books. Every weekend, my dad took me to the Tuckahoe Public Library to check out a bunch of books like *The Cricket in Times Square*, *Anastasia Krupnik*, *A Wrinkle in Time*, and *A Tree Grows in Brooklyn*. I'd devour them, finishing three or four chapter books a week. I read the entire Boxcar Children series in one summer. Camped out in our sunroom, I'd sprawl sideways in the faded navy-blue corduroy armchair, my legs dangling over the puffy armrest. The chair was so old that it probably had more mildew and mites inside than stuffing. I guess that's why Mom put it out in the sunroom. "The cure for mildew is sunlight," she always said.

But as a kid I didn't care about mildew, so it was my favorite place. There was a skylight in the slanted ceiling where you could look up to see the green leaves in the spring, reds and oranges in the fall. And in the winter: white sky and brown branch. During summertime, I'd spend all day in that gross blue chair eating Popsicles and reading books. The only sounds were turning pages or an occasional bird. A distant lawn mower. Such a nice kind of quiet. Before I ever wanted to be an actor, I wanted to be a writer because books were my favorite thing in the world.

I got my first big writing assignment in eighth grade. It was for Western Civilization class, and it had to be a minimum of ten pages. Most of the kids groaned about the length and schemed on formatting tricks to cheat it— bigger margins, different fonts, double spacing. But me? I was excited by the ten pages. A real writing assignment! And it was assigned by my favorite teacher, Mrs. Kantor.

Mrs. Kantor had the ballsy attitude of Elaine Stritch and the self-satisfied charm of Fran Drescher. Her short hair was dyed a dry blond, she wore good jewelry, and her chin was always tilted up as though she were balancing an exquisite charm on the tip of her nose. She spoke with a New York accent and a voice that sounded like cigarettes and the stiff part of Velcro. Her smile, like Robert DeNiro's, was shaped like a frown.

Her tough personality made her a legend in our school. She was the type of scary that was fun, like a Disney villainess—Cruella de Vil or Ursula in *The Little Mermaid*. When she gave you sass, you felt loved. She teased us with salacious stories to get us interested in history. She'd mention Catherine the Great, saying, "Oy, don't even get me started on what *she* did. I can't even say. You'll have to learn about it when you are older." There was no internet to look it up back then, so we giggled in hushed whispers about the rumor that Catherine the Great fucked horses. While the other teachers and staff seemed to fear Mrs. Kantor, the students loved her. The mix of intimidation and affection gave her a unique type of power. You could tell she enjoyed it too.

Her desk had fun things on it like a jar that said "The ashes of bad students" and a big bowl she filled with Tootsie Rolls or strawberry candies. She arranged her classroom like her personal fashion runway, beginning at the class-room door and ending at her desk. The desks were lined up on either side of the runway, facing in toward it. During class, she sashayed up and down it as she lectured, pivoting at each end, her pelvis jutting out, chest sunk in, braceleted wrist swaying to and fro as she taught us about the horrors of the Holocaust being caused by the charisma of Hitler. About how charisma could be deceptive.

The term paper she assigned us was on a Western histori-cal figure of our choice. Mrs. Kantor stressed the importance of the opening paragraph. She jokingly moaned about stu-dents' inability to write a compelling one: all facts, no flair. "You are all idiots who are lucky to have me," she exclaimed as we laughed, loving her more for her brash, affectionate mockery. *Yes! We are terrible! Haha!* To help us, she offered office hours before school to work with students on their opening paragraphs. You signed up for a fifteen-minute time slot. It wasn't mandatory but strongly suggested.

I never signed up because I was confident about my open-ing paragraph. I chose to write about Beethoven, because I thought the idea of a pianist losing his hearing was very dra-matic and cool. I began by describing an ocean of white roses and made Beethoven the single red rose among the sea of white, a dramatic metaphor praising the defiant beauty of those who stand out. In retrospect, the writing was indulgent and melodramatic, but it was fucking great for a twelve-year-old. I couldn't wait for her to read it.

A few days later, as the students were settling in before class, Mrs. Kantor asked me to step outside for a minute. There weren't any hallways at our school; the classrooms opened to a cement sidewalk that encircled a grass courtyard. I obeyed, following her out onto the sidewalk. I hadn't brought my coat with me; it was cold enough that you could see your breath. That morning, there was frost on the grass that made it look like crystals. Mrs. Kantor closed the door to the classroom, looked down at me, and said, "I think you plagiarized your term paper. You are not good enough to have written this."

She pointed to my opening paragraph.

The one I had been so proud of.

My head started spinning and the air was knocked out of my lungs. It was such a shock. I never imagined that I would be accused of plagiarism, because, well, *I hadn't plagiarized*. I felt scolded and scared. My favorite teacher had just told me "you are not good enough."

"I didn't!" I said, bursting into tears. And once the tears started, they wouldn't stop. I was crying so hard. I was only a kid, but rather than soothing me or calming me down, Mrs. Kantor narrowed her eyes and said, "Now I *know* you're guilty, because if you were innocent, you wouldn't cry. You would take it as a compliment. You're crying because you got caught!" And with that, she walked back into her classroom and slammed the door, leaving me alone on the sidewalk. I didn't know what to do. I couldn't run away; I wasn't that kind of student. I couldn't stay out in the cold either. So I had to walk back into the hushed classroom after her.

The students had settled in, waiting for class to start. And I had to walk down the stupid runway of her stupid classroom to get to my stupid desk. Crying.

The students were mystified, their faces a mixture of pity, curiosity, and alarm. Mrs. Kantor was scary-angry and began her lesson without addressing my tears. I tried to stop crying but I just . . . couldn't. My emotions have always been larger than my body. Trying to hold them back usually makes them worse. So I opened my textbook and bowed my head over it so my hair formed a curtain to hide the tears that were dropping down, wrinkling the pages. Though I tried to keep still, my body was shaking from the exertion it took to cry without sound.

Mitchell Hopewell sat at the desk next to mine. He was one of those genuinely good Christian boys. I didn't know him that well, but I will always remember the pathos and conflict on his face—he knew Mrs. Kantor would yell at him if he talked to me. But after a few minutes, he chose to comfort me anyway. To this day, when I try to think of a caring face, I often think of Mitchell in that moment. "Hey," he said, "it's okay . . ." He put his hand on my back, tried to reassure me, show me some kindness. This made Mrs. Kantor furious.

"Don't you touch her. Don't talk to her!" she snapped. "She needs to STOP CRYING." She turned to me and in a mocking, whiney voice said, "Your crying is an admission of guilt. If you hadn't plagiarized, you wouldn't be in this situation. If you had really written it, you would be proud. You would consider it a compliment. SO STOP CRYING."

At this point, I was full-on sobbing. I felt so helpless. What do you do when the truth is not enough? When someone's disbelief is enough to incriminate you?*

After class she told me she was going to be fair—she would check all the sources in my bibliography to find the proof of plagiarism, but if I just admitted it now, the punishment would be less severe. I think she was trying to scare me into confessing, but there was nothing to confess. In fact, her promising to check my bibliography made me feel a little hope, because I knew she wouldn't find anything. So I said, "I really did write it, Mrs. Kantor." She threw her hands up and walked away in a huff.

She didn't ever find any proof, but Mrs. Kantor was determined. So she did the meanest thing ever.

She got my class schedule and took time out of her day to go to all of my other classes. She marched me up to my teachers, thrust my paper in front of them, pointed to the

---

*Years later, I wrote a tweet for which I was accused of I was co-opting the *Believe Women* call of the #MeToo movement for self-serving purposes. At the time, I wasn't thinking of that at all . . . I was actually thinking about Mrs. Kantor's disbelief. It's a very old, tender wound that's easily triggered in me. It wasn't until later that I realized my poor word choice's overlap. I was glad to be made aware of it and am sorry and will do better next time.

opening paragraph, and asked, "Do you think Constance is good enough to have written this?"

No, said Mrs. Dean.

No, said Mr. Brantley.

No, said Mrs. Harrison.

No, said Mrs. Rogers.

She was so smug, turning to me after each one as if to say, *See?*

I was twelve years old.

She made me watch every one of my teachers say that I was not good enough.

Except Mr. Frizzell. Mr. Frizzell taught drama class, which had been my elective for the past two years. His name was pronounced fruh-ZELL. He looked like Santa Claus in Levi's and had the easy demeanor of a George Clooney type. Mrs. Kantor walked into his classroom, nose tilted up, and shoved my paper at him. "Do you think she is good enough to have written this?"

Mr. Frizzell read it quietly and handed it back without even looking at her. "Well, do you think she wrote it?" Mrs. Kantor demanded. Then, with the casualness of someone who had a class to teach, someone who couldn't be bothered with such a nonsense question, he said, "Of course she did." And he showed Mrs. Kantor the door.

Mrs. Kantor was unable to find anything to incriminate me. She gave me a C on the paper, explaining that it should have been an F, but since she didn't find the sources I had "stolen" from, she was being fair by *not* giving me an F. Instead, she took 20 points off for two run-on sentences.

I remember feeling tired when she handed my paper back. I accepted the grade. I think I even thanked her.

After that, I didn't want to be a writer anymore.

My parents never monitored me much in school, so I was able to keep the entire incident to myself. I couldn't tell them, not because of the grade . . . but because it was an *American* problem.

Parents are generally smarter and more experienced than their kids. But there's this thing that sometimes happens with the kids of immigrant parents. There's a tacit understanding that because your parents didn't grow up in America, they *don't get* American stuff. My sisters and I either *taught* our parents about American problems, or we just handled them ourselves. My parents would not have understood a Mrs. Kantor type—the charm of her brashness, the way it overpowered everything else. I also thought that she'd use their foreignness, their very accents, to discredit me further. Nonimmigrant Americans often equate accented English with a lack of intelligence. But my parents are educated and smart. They can *write* in English beautifully with clear grammar. But their spoken accents are strong to some. I knew Mrs. Kantor would hear their accents and think they were stupid. I wasn't going to let anyone think my parents were stupid. I had to protect them.

That's why I never told them.

Compared to other traumas I've been through, this one shouldn't have been so bad. But for some reason, it's the one that hurts the most. I've come back to it in therapy again and again, always crying fresh tears. Surprised that it still hurts, even after all these years.

The first time I addressed it in therapy was during my senior year of college. I decided that I needed to do something about it—prove myself, make her pay, get an apology . . . *something* to get it out of my system. I decided to call her.

I was twenty-one years old when I looked up Mrs. Kantor in the Richmond phone book. My heart was pounding as I dialed her number. The phone rang a few times before she picked up. Her Velcro voice and New York accent were unmistakable.

THE SCENE: SEEKING ATONEMENT FOR A VERY OLD WOUND

Constance sits on the floor of her college dorm room, phone in her lap, receiver to her ear, nervously tangling and untangling the coiled phone cord. Her heart racing, she clutches a piece of paper, on which she's written a prepared speech.

CONSTANCE
Hi, is this Mrs. Kantor?

MRS. KANTOR
Yes, speaking.

(Beat.)

> CONSTANCE
>
> Mrs. Kantor, who taught Western Civilization
> at Tuckahoe Middle School?

> MRS. KANTOR
>
> Yes, who's this?

> CONSTANCE
>
> You probably don't remember me.
> Constance Wu. I was your student, like,
> ten years ago.

> MRS. KANTOR
>
> Oh, well, sweetheart, I've had a lot of
> students over the years—

(Constance stands up, red-faced. Her hand shakes as she clutches the receiver.)

> CONSTANCE
>
> I wrote my term paper on Beethoven. The red
> rose in the sea of white. You didn't believe I
> wrote it. You said I plagiarized.

(Beat.)

> MRS. KANTOR
>
> Oh. Right. Yes, I remember.

(Constance half laughs, half cries, breathless. She begins reading from her prepared speech, as tears fall.)

CONSTANCE

(between gasps)

Well. I am calling. To tell you. Almost ten years after the fact. That I. Really wrote that paper. I . . . I wrote every single word. You were wrong! I didn't plagiarize. I wrote it, all of it. It was wrong of you to do that. Wrong to do that to a kid. How dare you. It hurt me. It still hurts me.

MRS. KANTOR

Well. That was so long ago, sweetie.

(Constance's pitch raises as her sentences build rapidly.)

CONSTANCE

But you need to know that I wrote it! I really wrote it! You said I wasn't good enough. It was wrong to say that to a kid! I was only twelve!

MRS. KANTOR

I'm not sure I said that.

CONSTANCE

Yes, you did! YOU DID. You made all the other teachers say it too!

MRS. KANTOR

Oh. Well . . . what was I supposed to do when
everyone else agreed with me? It's not my fault.

CONSTANCE

. . .

MRS. KANTOR

I didn't actually give you an F . . . if you
remember. I did what was fair since I couldn't
find where you plagiarized. But I remember
I did my due diligence. I made sure I checked
all the sources listed in your bibliography.
But sweetie . . . there was one book listed in
your bibliography that I couldn't find in the
school library . . . so I assumed that was the
book you plagiarized from. This was before
the internet; I couldn't just look up the book
and find it.

CONSTANCE

My . . . dad worked at VCU. I used that
library sometimes.

MRS. KANTOR

Ah! So that's it! That makes perfect sense. . . .
I didn't have access to that library! Well, I'm
glad that now we both understand!

CONSTANCE

W-w-wait. But . . . but I still wrote it.
I need you to know that.

(Mrs. Kantor changes the subject, talking over her with
enthusiasm, like a kindergarten teacher asking a
five-year-old what her favorite color is.)

MRS. KANTOR

And how have you been? Are you in
college now?

(Constance, feeling helpless and unheard, doesn't know
what to do other than answer her question.)

CONSTANCE

I . . . Um, yeah. Yes, I'm in college?

MRS. KANTOR

Good! Are you still singing? That was
always your *true* talent. I hope you are!

CONSTANCE

I . . . yes, a little? I still sing. But I mean,
I'm studying acting now. Like Shakespeare
and stuff.

MRS. KANTOR

Well, that's just wonderful! Good for you.
Best of luck.

(Mrs. Kantor hangs up the phone.)

After that phone call, I felt even worse.

One of the first things you learn in Method acting is called sense memory. Instead of dwelling on the emotions of an event, you recall the sensory parts—sound, touch, smell, taste, sight. Sense memories become the building blocks of your character history. When I first started writing this piece, I wrote like ten different drafts. Something didn't click. I couldn't figure out what I was trying to say or what the experience was trying to tell me.

So I did what actors do: I went back to the beginning with sense memory—the smell of the library books and the mildewy blue chair. The color of moving leaves as seen through the skylight. That special summer quiet. The pleasure of a good book. Those sticky, sweet twin Popsicles that broke into halves. Mrs. Kantor's voice, that gray sidewalk, the way my breath looked in the cold air. The heat of my tears and the sting that pulled them out of me. Mitchell's hand on my back, his voice trying to comfort me. My cheeks burning in shame as every teacher said they didn't believe in me. The way my heart soared when Mr. Frizzell said, *"Of course she did."*

Before a play begins, the theater is filled with sound. People chatting, finding their seats, flipping through their playbills. It's a pleasant, low hum. There's always a moment, right before the curtain rises, when the hum stills, without cue—as if everyone in the theater has made a silent agreement: *it's time*. Then the lights go down and the play begins. Whenever this happens, I often find myself fighting back tears of joy. I'm just so goddamn happy to be in a theater. Every time, I wonder why it's the one place where I feel safest, most alive, and in love with the world.

As I went through the sense memories of that traumatic day back in eighth grade, suddenly it all *made* sense. Why this, out of all my life experiences, was the most formative. Why I couldn't ever let it go. Why it meant so much. Why I stopped wanting to be a writer, and fled to the safe home of the theater.

Because while there was Mrs. Kantor, there was also Mr. Frizzell.

I never realized the significance of that until now. Isn't that crazy? I'd spent so long dwelling on the hurt that I hadn't been able to look beyond to see how it *helped me*. How it made me who I am today. It took me more than two decades to realize how significant it was that the only teacher who believed me was my drama teacher. And look what it led me to—a career, an entire life! So *that's* why I became an actor. Of course I did.

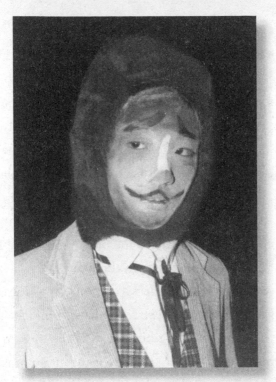

Playing Mole in *The Wind in the Willows*

Exploring an Orange

It was my first-ever theater audition. I'd tagged along only because my friend Lauren wanted me to and I liked being around Lauren, liked how different she was from me. The quiet seriousness of her face. The gentleness of her hands on objects. The way she and her mother had a language that didn't require words or even eye contact. Lauren wanted me to come with her because she didn't want to go by herself. So, after school one day, her mom picked us up and took us to audition for the play *A Little Princess*.

It was a children's play, based on the book by Frances Hodgson Burnett. Except for Lauren, I didn't know any of the other kids at that audition. It wasn't a school play but a *community theater* play—any kid in town could audition. All the auditioning girls sat with their moms in the fluorescent-lit rec room of a public school (not our school) on those hard orange chairs. Remember those chairs? The kind that look like the seats in the seventies-era idea of a spaceship? Acrylic and round with strong steel legs that were always a little uneven and wobbly. I used to try to see if I could hold my body still in such a way that the chair was balancing on only two diagonal legs. When I got it to balance, hovering for more than a second, it felt like I had made magic.

That day, I was focused not on the chair but on the audition. I'd never been to one before. We got to see all the other girls' auditions, because they had us perform our monologues in front of each other, like an audience. Every girl got the same monologue. It was a simple, sweet scene where the main character, Sara, is alone in her room when she finds a little present from a friend. Sara is talking to her doll, named Emily. As the girls went up, one by one, to the front of the room to recite it, most of them were stiff and nervous. Shaking as they read from the paper clutched in their hands. Some were overly polished, like news anchors or pageant queens. No one stood out.

As a kid, I never wanted to stand out. I'd always preferred to *fit in*—I wore the clothing styles that other girls wore, I adopted the mannerisms and slang of teens on TV, even modeled my handwriting after another girl's in my class. You were a weirdo if you stood out. But as I watched those girls audition, I realized that here you were *supposed* to stand out. It wouldn't make you a weirdo because it wasn't you; it was the character. Those weren't your words; they were the playwright's. Wow! To me, that seemed like freedom. Why were these girls so stiff when they could be free? When my name was called, I felt a highly charged sense of purpose.

I practically fucking bled onstage. I went full-on Sally

Field crying over Julia Roberts's death in *Steel Magnolias*. I made a goddamn *scene* of it. Clutching my chest and wringing my hands to the heavens as I fell to my knees, weeping: "Oh Papa, oh Emily, I have a friend . . . I have a friend!" I, um, definitely took it overboard. But the response from the audience was awe and applause. For what felt like the first time in my life, I wasn't being punished or ridiculed for having big feelings. I was being *applauded*.

I got a part in the play! Back in the nineties, where we lived was predominantly white, so I was the only Asian kid in the cast. Sure, *A Little Princess* was a period piece that took place in 1800s England, but I was still cast in the play, despite not looking like a British white girl, because community theater isn't about box office or authenticity or even art, really. Community theater is about just that: the community. And in friendly Richmond, our family had always been welcomed as part of the community.

For the next eight years of my life, until I went away for college, I was always doing a play. I got to know all the local theater kids. I remember Casey and Kelly, two home-schooled sisters with *fairy-tale* hair. Long and auburn, it curled in shiny ringlets down their backs. Casey was the older sister, pretty and reserved, always close to her mom. Kelly was the younger one, bouncy and enthusiastic. She and I were often double cast in the same part because we were the same size and had the same spirit. She was delighted by random, surprising things—like when Robbie (one of the other kid actors who all the girls had crushes on) spilled crumbs on the floor and tried to clean them up with a dry paper towel. Kelly laughed so hard she could barely breathe. "He tried . . . to clean it . . . with . . . a *dry paper towel!*" Her joy was so contagious that Robbie and I started laughing too—and once we started we couldn't stop. It was one of those nights of rehearsals where we were all so happy, the laughter burst out of us like songs in a musical, or a sneeze.

Everyone's families participated in community theater. The moms brought their sewing machines to the rec room next to our rehearsal room and made our costumes. My mom was a social butterfly and a great sewer, so she enjoyed it too. Loved chatting with the other moms, poring over scraps of fabric from Jo-Ann, trading pinking shears and patterns. My dad recorded all my plays, camcorder in hand, his lens always focused on me, even during scenes where I was just in the background. "Dad, you got to focus on the story, not just me!" I'd later protest (though I was secretly pleased). None of my three sisters were artsy types, but they still came to my performances to cheer me on. Even my next-door neighbors Betty and Syd came to every opening night and brought me flowers.

My favorite role I played was Mole in *The Wind in the Willows.* He was one of a quartet of animal characters in the play: Toad was vain and reckless. Rat was relaxed and leisurely. Badger was grumpy and gruff. And Mole was timid and polite, hiding himself in an underground burrow. He was shy and terrified and relied on his friends for courage. I felt like I *understood* Mole. I exaggerated my shyness like Winnie-the-Pooh's Piglet. *Oh d-d-d-d-dear!* I wore thick gray makeup all over my face, black around the edges. I painted on eyebrows that curved up in the middle to make me look worried because Mole was always worried. I painted a pink tip on my nose, and whiskers too. My mom sewed me a black faux-fur mole head that fastened under my chin with a Velcro strap. My costume consisted of a white button-up shirt, a plaid vest, pleated trousers, and a thick corduroy blazer. I came dressed correct, because even though Mole was shy, he was still a proper Englishmole. And oh! Mole wore sunglasses because the sun was too bright for his underground mole eyes.

My biggest role was in *The Magician's Nephew*, a play based on one of the Chronicles of Narnia. I played Polly Plummer, the lead. Digory, the male lead, was played by a cute boy named Mark. The play had a scene where Polly and Digory enter with a candle, and we used a real candle! During rehearsal breaks, Mark and I loved playing with the candle. We ran our fingers quickly through the flame. Blew it out repeatedly to watch the smoke curl. Dripped the wax on our fingertips, peeling it off to inspect our fingerprints.

The actress playing Queen Jadis was an adult. It made me feel so cool to be acting with a *grown-up*. She was blond and pretty and tall. She listened to what I had to say as if I were her equal; she took me seriously, told me I made smart observations. No one ever talked down to you in community theater, even if you were little.

On Saturdays, we had matinee and evening shows. Between shows we'd hang out in the chorus room. There would be a few two-liter bottles of soda and Cheetos or Oreos or something. Fun kid snacks. Sometimes we got pizza delivered. Cell phones and laptops didn't exist back then, so we brought our own activities. We played lots of card games. I'd sprawl out on the floor, lying on my stomach, feet kicked up to the ceiling, calves swinging to and fro like a dog's tail. Propped up on my elbows, a slice of pizza in one hand, a hand of cards in the other. Community theater was where I learned to shuffle and back shuffle—a skill I got pretty terrific at. To this day, shuffling cards is one of my favorite ways to relax.

If we tired of playing cards, someone might play the piano, and someone else might sing show tunes (always harmonizing, of course). Or you could read a book without being bothered. Most theater kids like reading, so there were always at least two or three kids reading. We'd trade books by writers like Lois Lowry, Judy Blume, and Madeleine L'Engle. Or we'd read choose-your-own-adventure books out loud to each other, trying out all the options to hear the different ways the story could end.

Most of the community theater shows were directed by a woman in her thirties named Becki. She was short and soft, with fine brown hair and a facial expression like that of a friendly, curious chipmunk. She wore clear plastic glasses and pastel-colored clothing.

I learned so many things from Becki: What downstage and upstage are, and why they are called that (because stage floors used to be built tilted downward to the audience). Why it is so important to say, "Thank you, ten," when the stage manager gives you your ten-minute warning. To call *it* the Scottish Play. Why it's bad luck to whistle in a theater. I learned that, even if I *thought* I would remember the blocking of a scene (should be easy, right?), I wouldn't. You *had* to write it down. I learned about stage makeup (Ben Nye, always Ben Nye), and we all did our own makeup.

Before every show, Becki pulled us in for a group exercise she called an "amoeba." The entire cast stood in a circle. We closed our eyes, held hands around the circle for a long, silent moment, just breathing together. In that quiet, you could hear the room fill up with gratitude. It almost felt like prayer. "An amoeba is a single-celled organism," Becki would say. "We are an amoeba."

There was one tech rehearsal when Becki taught us how to "find your light." It's when a spotlight hits the dark stage, and you step into it to speak your monologue. There is a sweet spot of the light that's different for every person. It varies based on the spotlight's angle and the actor's height. The key to finding it, she said, is when the warmth hits you just right and brightness is all around. Becki made sure we all knew how to find our light.

I continued pursuing my love of theater into college, exclusively applying to schools with classical theater conservatory programs. They were BFA programs, not BA programs, so academic transcripts were kind of an afterthought. You *auditioned* for college—two 2-minute monologues, one contemporary and one classical, and a third backup in case they wanted to see more. For my contemporary, I did Arlie's frog monologue from Marsha Norman's *Getting Out*. For my classical, Cleopatra's dream speech from Shakespeare's *Antony and Cleopatra*. My backup was from *The Woolgatherer* by William Mastrosimone. I was accepted to a few different schools, but SUNY Purchase Conservatory of Theatre Arts and Film was the one I could afford, which was great, because it was also one of the best back then. Their acting program was highly competitive; they accepted only around twenty-five people for their incoming freshman class (which they called a "company").

It was an unconventional college curriculum. Conservatory classes didn't have written tests or papers. We had required yoga class three times a week at 7:15 a.m. (a painful wake-up time for an undergrad), and if you missed more than three yoga classes a semester, you were kicked out of the program. The threat of being kicked out was constant because they made yearly cuts! Twenty-five students are already a small freshman company, but the program was designed so that it would become even smaller. If you were in danger of being cut, they put you on probation. At any given time, half the company was on probation. By the time we graduated, only fifteen actors remained. This wasn't Mole wearing a fur cap sewn by Mom. No. This was structure, craft, discipline. It was Tennessee Williams, August Wilson, Eugene O'Neill, Bertolt Brecht. We studied the great teachers— Meisner and Boleslavsky and Stanislavsky and Strasberg and Edith Skinner and Kristin Linklater. Performed Chekhov scenes wearing rehearsal skirts. Had classes like Stage Combat and Clowning and Balinese Mask. At conservatory, acting was considered an *honorable* profession.

I wasn't cut, but I was always on probation . . . for bad acting! And I *was* bad . . . I came from the big, exaggerated world of community theater, so my acting was presentational, cheesy. Rather than feeling my character's emotions, I indicated them in an effort to impress my teachers with my understanding of the scene. The teachers were unimpressed. They didn't care about hard work or character analysis; they wanted blood.

"*Get the fuck out of your head!*" my acting teacher screamed at me. My fellow company members yelled it at me too. *Get the fuck out of your head!* We screamed that phrase all the time, at ourselves, at each other, at the goddamn walls. The screaming wasn't hostile, but more of a rousing battle cry, like that of an athlete rooting for her teammate. I was screamed at for not going deep enough (too cerebral!) or for trying to go *too* deep (pushing!). We wrote fierce quotes all over the studio walls in chalk: *Be real. Get the fuck out* *of your head. Go deep. An ounce of behavior is worth a pound of words.* The men in my company were particularly passionate. If something felt really deep and intense, they would say things like "Blau! That shit is fucking hot!" as they jumped from the slanted window ledges, barefoot, like wild animals. For some reason, a lot of the boys loved to hold the rubber prop gun to their head while putting on tough, dire faces, pretending to be on edge or tragic. They were important; they were going to take the world by storm.*

We spent most of college barefoot. Voice class began with lying on the floor, barefoot, eyes closed, massaging our solar plexuses and humming as the teacher walked around our supine bodies, instructing us to free our voices. We rolled to our sides and stood up from the ground, unraveling vertebra by vertebra while murmuring *"Hmm-uh. Huh-hummm-uh."* We massaged our jaws to relax the muscles and then violently shook our fists in the air to loosen the jaw to a wobble. We raised our arms to the sky and dropped them down in fists, beating our breasts as we bellowed *"AHHHHHHHH"* to free our chest resonance. Nasal resonance was activated by

---

*Decades later, when I was filming a TV show where my character had to shoot a gun, I remember being shocked and terrified that they used real guns on set. I thought of the boys in my conservatory putting the rubber gun to their heads for fun. Even though the real guns on set were loaded with blanks or dummy rounds, it was still intimidating. I was grateful for the armorer on that show, who shone a flashlight into the gun before every take to show me: "empty chamber, empty mag, empty magwell." Or if he had to load the gun, how he shook every single bullet next to both his ear and my ear before loading it to listen for the rattle inside ensuring that it was a dummy round.

vigorously rubbing our sinuses while vocalizing "N-N-NAY, WAY, M-M-M-MY, HI" in a whiney-type voice. We sang out "KEEEE-eeee" like opera singers over and over, to open our head voices.

In speech class, we learned to drop our regionalisms and adopt a mid-Atlantic accent when doing classical plays, which was then considered the standard according to Edith Skinner's *Speak with Distinction*. For a lot of folks, this class got emotional. Jerry, a kid from the Bronx, once blew up in anger when he wasn't able to say "water" the way the teacher instructed him. "You're saying it wrong," our speech teacher insisted, refusing to move on until he got it "right." But Jerry couldn't hear the difference. She drilled him ruthlessly, for an unreasonable amount of time until he finally kicked his chair over in frustration and stormed out of the room. Loretta once broke down in tears over long-vowel sounds. She was from Texas, and the Britishy-sounding dialect made her feel embarrassed and self-conscious. I didn't have a strong regionalism and I've always had a good ear for sound, so speech class wasn't difficult for me. But I understood Jerry's and Loretta's frustration. It feels bad when someone says you are not speaking right—to be heard not for what you're saying but for how you're saying it.

My favorite class was sophomore-year Shakespeare. I loved it because of our teacher, Jennie. Jennie was pretty and curvy with red hair and empathic eyes. She was a graduate of Yale School of Drama. Jennie was on our side—she never put a single student on probation. When Jerry told her about his frustration at being told he was saying "water" *wrong*, she told us a story of when she was in drama school, and her voice teacher had tried to correct how she said her name. "It's not Jin-nee. . . . It's *Jeh-nee*," her teacher had said. Well. Jennie wasn't having *that*. "It's my name and I decide how to say it. My name is Jin-nee," she proclaimed. We adored her. She was defiant and radical and full of love. She brought her passion for Shakespeare into the studio like a burst of fresh air.

My entire college career, most of my teachers assigned me only ingenue roles—young, feminine romantic-lead types. When I asked to play more complex roles, my teachers balked at the request, telling me I needed to understand my "type." Jennie was the only teacher who believed I could be more than an ingenue. In her class, she assigned me the role of Lady Macbeth.

In preparation, she had us do an exercise where we printed our monologues on paper, and then cut each word out with scissors and put them in a ziplock bag. In complete silence, we lay down on the floor barefoot and pulled our monologue's words out of the ziplock one at a time. In silence, we thought about each word for a long time. I remember pulling out the word "hope." *Hope . . . hope . . . hope*. I thought of every way I had known that word. What hope meant, what it felt like. How it felt when I was a kid and used to have such hope. How it felt to lose it. The hopes I had—the ones proclaimed, and the ones I was too embarrassed to share. What other people's hopes were for me. How their hope made me feel guilty sometimes. How it felt to see someone else with so much hope during times when I couldn't conjure it in myself. Then I thought about what "hope" meant to Lady Macbeth. We did that with each word in the ziplock. It took forever, but Jennie made sure we took *time* for language. Until that exercise, I'd never realized how one little word could hold so much. Exploring the personal, emotional history of language was formative for me.

The first time I started Lady Macbeth's speech, I was terrified. How could I get to a place of such ruthlessness? I couldn't even begin the speech I was so paralyzed. Seeing this, Jennie activated. She came up to me and grasped both of my hands, her eyes blazing into mine with a fire that felt like faith. *If you fall, I will catch you*, her eyes said, and suddenly I was roaring into Lady Macbeth: *"Was the hope drunk / wherein you dressed yourself? Hath it slept since? / And wakes it now to look so green and pale / At what it did so freely? From this time, / Such I account thy love!"* It was the first time I truly "got out of my head" and lost myself in Lady Macbeth. Everything felt like it *dropped in*, and what had once seemed so hard didn't take effort at all. . . . It took a freedom and surrender that I discovered in the safety of Jennie's faith, her hands holding mine. It was a thrilling moment.

———————

In freshman year acting class, we spent an entire month doing animal work. It's a typical conservatory course where you find the animal in a character and bring it out in the performance. There's a common actor's lore that Anthony Hopkins used animal work—a snake—for his role in *The Silence of the Lambs*. For the assignment, we would each choose a specific animal to study. And then we'd . . . *become* that animal. This was before YouTube, so we studied the real thing. Our teacher, Eulalie, took us to the Bronx Zoo to spend the afternoon observing our animal. I chose a kangaroo, studying its movement, facial expression, behavior, vocalization. After a few weeks we went into the acting studio to battle each other as our chosen animals. Monkey vs. Horse. Lizard vs. Bear. Eulalie lived for intensity, so the more guttural and animalistic the encounter, the better. She wanted *commitment*. But back then, animal work made me self-conscious. I was too immature to fully commit; it embarassed me and I wasn't any good at it. Some people were great at it— I remember Dorothy did some kind of monkey that used its own poop as a weapon, flinging it at enemies. When she went into her animal battle onstage, she pantomimed the poop with her hand cupped beneath her butt and threw it at her "opponent," who faked being hit by it, the way you'd fake getting a stage slap. I still remember Dorothy's face, eyes wide and wild, body squatted and loose, arms waving above her head as she screeched and threw imaginary poop.

Animal work is hard. In order to drop into it, you have

to abandon judgment and self-consciousness. Most people can't do that, so they make fun of it. Because, yeah, waving your arms and flinging imaginary poop looks ridiculous. But for that animal in the wild, it's not a joke; it is survival. Dorothy was very brave to go to that place completely. She wasn't worrying about her own embarrassment, nor was she exploiting the animal's behavior to milk her audience for a laugh. It wasn't about *her* at all; it was about her animal and its survival. She honored her animal. Took the time to do right by it.

It would be years before I became emotionally mature enough to commit like that. Outside the bubble of community theater, the world often mocks sincerity and commitment— *especially* in Hollywood. There are entire genres of comedy devoted to ridiculing passionate people. LA cool kids, New York cynics—if they had seen my audition for *A Little Princess* or Dorothy's animal work? They'd have laughed, turned it into a joke. That's why it was so comforting to be in the safety of that first audition room when I was a kid— big feelings were rewarded. Or in Shakespeare class, where I was free to give meaning and passion to language without eye rolls or jeers. I've spent half my life trying to shrink my big feelings, and when I was unable to do that, I spent the other half trying to not be ashamed of them. I still struggle with this.

Remembering my first audition, for *A Little Princess*, makes me kinda sad. I am sad I'm not that kid anymore. Sure, she was a terrible actor, but she wasn't afraid. Her overblown weeping ecstasy of an audition might have been messy and large. But she took it seriously. That's why I almost didn't confess this next part . . . because it's too big, too emotional. Too *too*. I *know* it is. It will be very easy to ridicule, and it will hurt my feelings when somebody does. But fuck it. This is my book, my stage, my story.

So here is my confession. My feelings are so big, an orange made me weep. Yup. A goddamn piece of fruit.

One day we spent an entire acting class "exploring an orange." It was a sense memory exercise, one of the foundations of Method acting. We each brought our own orange to class, where we were instructed to examine its elements through our senses. *Two hours* of only you, the quiet, and the orange.

We did this class outside because it can get messy. It was a brisk fall day, the sun bright and clear. The air smelled like crisp leaves and cold in a way that made you think of the worms and bugs underground. Our chairs were spread haphazardly on the grass. The exercise, like all things in drama school, began with the process of relaxation. In complete silence, starting from our toes up to the tops of our heads, we isolated each muscle in the body, tensing and releasing until our arms were dangling by our sides, heads collapsed backward, slack jaws gaping open. Legs splayed out like rag dolls.

Then, enters the orange . . .

I put my ear close to the peel and break it, hearing its faint sigh as the peel gives. I feel the cool oils that mist out when I twist the peel. My fingers get sticky but in a clean way. I taste its sweetness, feel my tongue prickle at its tang. I smell the sharp brightness of the juice and the acrid bitterness of the peel. The senses flood me with memories and suddenly I am living in them again. I remember a quiet summer afternoon when I was a kid where I was all alone in the house peeling an orange at the kitchen table and feeling sad and didn't know why I was sad. Then I'm picturing a knife cleanly slicing through an orange as my mom taught me to cut them, not in line with the stem, but perpendicular to it, because it made for prettier slices. Her smile, proud, as she held it up to show me the perfect triangle wedges within the slice. I think of the listless oranges you got with the check at some Chinese restaurants, and how I loved reading my Chinese horoscope on those paper placemats even though it was always the same. I remember how orange was my favorite flavor Popsicle when I was a kid and how those Popsicles looked when you put them up to the sunlight. How good and cold they tasted on a hot summer day.

I consider all the times I had an orange without ever really looking at it. I think about how the orange made its way to me, picturing the truck it traveled in, and if the roads were dusty on the journey. I imagine the sound that the tree's leaves and branches made every time an orange was plucked from it. *Pull pluck rustle pull pluck rustle.* Maybe that's the only sound in a quiet grove. Or maybe there's tinny music playing out of a radio. I wonder who chose the music. This fruit was picked off a branch by a person. Did she choose the music? I wonder about her life—what's her favorite holiday? What do her hands look like? Her skin? Her smile? I imagine how her face warms and relaxes when she looks at her children and then her grandchildren. I wonder what she does on a Sunday afternoon. I wonder if she has any pain in her body from all the work.

Then I step back and see the whole orange tree and it is so lush and wide and wonderful! I can feel its years. How many years did it take that tree to get so big, to bear such fruit? How many seasons has it known, how many people have plucked its fruit? How many ladders have leaned against it? I think about that tree and how it is rooted in the same earth I stand on and how I can move my body all over the earth. The tree can't move from its roots, but its fruit can. So in a way that tree *has* moved to me through a quiet grove and a woman's hand and a truck on a dusty road to the dining hall, where I got it out of a ceramic bowl and brought it to my acting class, where I am tasting it and the juice drips down my chin and it's bright and wet and sweet and sharp. I suddenly feel a part of that orange, that tree, that woman who plucked it. It feels like a community of the world, and I'm connected to all of it, like Becki's amoeba exercise. *We are an amoeba,* she told us. And then I remember Becki and community theater and the excitement before the curtain went up. I remember being a happy kid, how it felt to be a happy kid. I mourn that kid a little bit. And then I am flooded with gratitude and grief and love and hope and memory. And it pierces my heart with a tender, exquisite pain as I float on the most delicate magic in the world, and suddenly, I find myself crying because I realize that this orange is a miracle. This orange, and the opportunity to explore it. What a privilege to be an actor, to examine life in this way. To take the time to do right by our animals.

Playing Polly Plummer in *The Magician's Nephew*

Community theater with Becki

Welcome to Jurassic Park

Mary Martin had a waterbed at her house. It was in her big sister's room. Mary and I were around eight years old, and we were best friends. The waterbed fascinated us. We rolled our twiggy bodies all over it to hear it slosh. Or lay flat on our backs, pretending to be at sea as our bodies undulated. We did that until her sister kicked us out, when we'd retreat to Mary's room to draw pictures in our shared diary or make friendship bracelets out of bright embroidery floss. If it was a nice day, we went to the backyard and did gymnastics on the lawn. Roundoff-back-handsprings or front and back walkovers. We both loved gymnastics and took classes together at the YMCA. The uneven bars were our favorite. Mary could do a glide kip, and I could do a sole circle catch.

Mary's house was food heaven for a kid. Her mom made us yummy stuff like mashed potatoes and Hamburger Helper. It was so good—hot and salty and soft. Her house had lots of treats too: cream-filled chocolate cupcakes with white icing looped on top, Gushers fruit snacks, Fruit by the Foot, a plastic keg of cheese ball puffs. Capri Sun or SunnyD to drink.

Our birthdays were only a few days apart, so she and I had

double birthday parties for a couple of years. We rented out an entire roller-skating rink (it was cheap back then, especially since our moms split the cost) and invited everyone in our grade, even the kids who weren't in our class, which made us very popular. We each had our own sheet cake at the parties. One year, hers was decorated with icing in curly green lines with clusters of purple dots to look like a grapevine. I thought it was so neat, those purple icing dots as grapes, so the next year, I made sure to get a grapevine cake. For a present one year, I got her some gymnastic bar grips—soft gray leather with a silver wrist buckle; they protected your palms from ripped calluses on the uneven bars. Mary was ecstatic. She got me a white stuffed bunny, which I still have today. I named her Cottontail. I don't love admitting this, but I still sleep with Cottontail every night.

Mary got her first watch—a pink-and-black sports watch with a woven nylon band and a large plastic case. It had a digital display and "Waterproof" written on the side (we dipped it in water—it was true!). I wanted whatever she had so I bought the same watch, but in a different color. Mine had a purple band and a white case with a contrasting teal line that went around the display. Both of our watches had Indiglo light displays—better than the side light that my dad's digital watch had . . . because Indiglo was lit from within. In bed at night, I'd push the Indiglo button over and over again. Every time the screen lit up in the dark, I felt a small surge of happiness.

Mary's house looked so different from mine. Besides the

waterbed and the snacks, there were also decorative pillows that I didn't learn were called "throw pillows" until I was an adult. Their plates and cups and bowls all matched. Their utensils too. Her kitchen had things like a toaster oven and a ceramic cookie jar with the word "cookies" painted on it. She had cable TV and a Barbie Dreamhouse. On the wall by the stairwell, framed school pictures of Mary and her sister smiled down at you. There was a picture for every year, so you could see them grow up as you climbed the stairs.

My family's kitchen had appliances like a rice cooker and water boiler. Stained Tupperware was stacked in piles on the counter next to jugs of dried mushrooms and grease-covered bottles of sauce. Our dishes and cups were a mismatched collection of garage sale finds. Plastic yogurt cups, cleaned out and reused for drinking cups, overwhelmed the cupboards. We had snacks like nori or red bean–filled mochi (or "mwa-gee" as my mom called it) or shrimp chips or pineapple cake. My entire childhood we never had cable TV.

But Mary never made me feel different. She didn't care that we didn't eat Hamburger Helper. Mary *liked* coming over for dinner, because of the rice! While my sisters and I thought rice was bland and obligatory, Mary *loved* it. She asked to put butter on hers, which we never did in our family, but my mom was happy to oblige. She was glad to see Mary enjoying her food, rather than hearing her daughters' usual groans. I remember how Mary swung and kicked her legs in her chair, practically dancing, as she gobbled up all her buttered rice and then asked for more.

Still, I was often embarrassed to have her over. Embarrassed of our house and how it was different. I thought Mary's house was the right way to be American, and my house was the wrong way. But Mary liked being at my house. She didn't even notice that it was different. Even though I grew up in conservative white suburbs, it wasn't the people who made me feel different; it was the TV. The houses on TV shows and movies all looked like Mary's. None of them looked like mine.

Asian Americans use the word "assimilation" a lot. It's kind of a fancy word for fitting in. Like lots of kids, I wanted to fit in. I was born in America, and I wanted to feel like I was supposed to be here. That my birthplace wasn't an accident. When American things like Thanksgiving or the Fourth of July happened, my sisters and I had to "teach" our parents: "Mom you're supposed to do it this way," I'd grumble. Or "Dad, you don't do it like that here." My parents had grown up in another country; they had another culture. Mom and Dad were easygoing types who never pushed their culture on us, so when we "taught" them what they were supposed to do, they didn't mind following our lead.

Over the years, I ended up assimilating very well. I did all the normal American stuff like cheerleading and talent shows and sleepover parties. I was accepted. It might have just been good Southern manners, but no one ever mentioned my being Asian. But then I'd be at a sleepover party, watching TV, when an Asian character would come on-screen. While none of the other girls ever said anything, my face always burned with shame, *especially* if that character spoke with an

Asian accent. I didn't want to be associated with them. I had done such a good job of fitting in and I didn't want the dumb TV character to ruin it. It was like in that movie *Jurassic Park* when they figured out the T. rex *can't see you if you don't move.* Anytime an Asian brought attention to their Asian-ness on TV, it was like they were running around in front of a T. rex. *Shut up! Go away!* I wanted to yell at them. *Stop making us look bad.* I spent the next twenty years of my life trying to avoid being seen by T. rexes.

Then came *Fresh Off the Boat.* *FOTB* would be the first American network TV show in more than twenty years to center an Asian American family's story. It was inspired by Eddie Huang's memoir of the same name. Eddie, like me, was an Asian American kid who grew up in all-white suburbia. But he'd had a very different experience. He hadn't always fit in, and his parents were strict, not easygoing like mine. I was cast in the role of his mom, Jessica Huang. When I got the part, I felt a mixture of happiness and uncertainty. I was elated to have an acting job, but *FOTB* hit a lot of soft spots:

1. It was a mainstream comedy, and I'd always considered myself a serious, dramatic actress.

2. My character was a mom, ten years older than I was, which, I'll admit, was a blow to my vanity.

3. The softest spot of all was her Asian-ness—her demeanor, her values, her accent. She wasn't trying to avoid the T. rex; she was taunting it.

Because *Fresh Off the Boat* wasn't race-neutral. It was race-*relevant*.

———————

The media had conflicting feelings about it too. Because the show was historic, it came with anticipation and media scrutiny that I wasn't used to. A lot of the commentary came from Asian American folks themselves who seemed to alternate between excitement and dread, support and hatred. There was expectation, defensiveness, pressure, anxiety. People hated and loved it before it even came out—simply based on a thirty-second trailer. Because I'd spent my twenties more worried about rent than representation, I admittedly didn't know much about it. But suddenly, there I was in the thick of it. I spent that first year simultaneously feeling afraid, happy, defensive, proud. And uncertain. Always uncertain.

The feeling of that experience reminds me of the time I jumped off a cliff in Hawaii. It was a rocky cliff over a swimming hole at the end of the Road to Hana. I had seen children, teens, and adults doing it, plunging into the water below. It was very high. There was a rock that jutted out from the cliff maybe halfway down. If you dropped straight down, it looked like you might hit it. So you *had* to take a running start and leap to avoid it.

I've always been a thrill-seeker. I love roller coasters, sky-diving, scary movies. But roller coasters were controlled by someone else. Skydiving was tandem. Movies had endings. On this cliff in Hawaii, it was just you and the elements.

Shivering in my wet bathing suit, I climbed to the top to try it. I chickened out several times. I'd inch toward the cliff's edge and peek down, psyching myself out before retreating on all fours, trying to stay close to the ground. Waving other people to go ahead of me. Dread and possibility clanging in my chest like wind chimes. Dread because death was dancing below (that rock jutting out halfway down!). And possibility because I had never actually done it so I had no idea how it would feel. I knew the only way I'd ever do it was if I abandoned all preparation and surrendered to my natural impulsivity. Without thinking, before I even realized I was doing it, I said *fuck it* and started running full speed to the edge of the cliff. I ran so fast that neither my body nor my brain could stop the momentum. There was no choice but to leap.

I landed in the water.

Not only was *Fresh Off the Boat* a success, it was critically acclaimed. But there was a lot of criticism, too. The word "stereotype" got thrown around a lot, especially by Asian Americans themselves. "Aren't you perpetuating stereotypes by playing a tiger mom?" "Why do you have to have a stereotypical accent?" They all seemed to be saying: *Don't you know that you're in Jurassic Park?* It brought back the feelings I had as a kid, where I wanted to yell at the TV: *SHUT UP, GO AWAY. Stop making me look bad. I don't want to be associated with someone who sounds like my parents.*

That's when I realized that my whole life, I'd let someone

else's ignorant ridicule of my parents matter more than my actual, lived experience of them. To lots of people, sure, my parents' accents sound like stereotypes. But to me? They're my parents.

I've heard a lot of Asian actors say, "I refuse to play stereotypical roles. I want to choose roles that could be played by anyone." They say that "success" will be when our Asian-ness isn't a part of the story, when we get cast in "non-stereotypical" roles. I do not subscribe to this idea of success. That career ethos, that desire to shut down Asian stereotypes, is a reaction to a Hollywood standard that was created by people who do not know us. I got into acting to be creative, not reactive. There will always be people who don't get it. You don't make art for them, so why let their ignorant ridicule inform your artistic choices?

There are real people who genuinely embody stereotypical attributes—they're our mothers and fathers, our uncles and aunts, our brainy cousins—I don't want to hide their voices or their stories. They are human too. Stereotypes are not harmful for their mere existence; they're harmful for their *reduction* of a person or group. Stereotyping reduces a person to his most obvious attributes, and then exploits that reduction. In many ways, I think that previously stereotyped roles deserve *more* representation . . . because Hollywood really did them a disservice the first go round. That's why I *want* to see great Asian American actors in accented, previously stereotyped roles—because I know what great actors can do. They give a character flesh, bones, history, heart. *Expanding* them, not reducing them. Then, instead of being embarrassed of those stereotypical attributes, we can humanize and celebrate them. What's so embarrassing about an accent? Our parents have accents because they know two languages. Let's be proud of that. How many white Americans can say the same? When a great actor refuses to play previously stereotyped roles, I worry that their proud proclamation of that choice actually *reduces* our humanity. When our reactivity to old wounds renders us ashamed to the point of objection or repudiation, it reinforces the mainstream's ignorant theory that the people who embody those stereotypes are inherently shameful. Or at the very least, uncool. Unassimilated. It's fearing a T. rex, when Jurassic Park isn't even real.

There will always be someone who laughs at the wrong thing. In more than a hundred episodes of *FOTB*, there were zero scripted jokes about Jessica's Asian accent. But some people still laughed at it. That's okay. We all have our little unconscious prejudices. And there will always be idiots. True artists don't cater their choices to accommodate the idiots. True artists just create something beautiful out of whatever materials they have. They don't care if the idiots don't "get" it. I shouldn't call them idiots. They're not. They're not T. rexes either. They're just people who don't know because they haven't seen a ton. And they haven't seen a ton because we aren't letting ourselves be seen. *They can't see us if we don't move.*

Baking cookies with Betty

Betty and Syd attending my Brownie Girl Scout graduation

Betty and Syd

The neighborhood I grew up in was a friendly one, made up of mostly white folks. Even though my family was Asian American, we always felt welcomed. In fact, when we first moved into the neighborhood, there were never fewer than six welcome pies or cakes in our kitchen at all times. For weeks, neighbors stopped by to introduce themselves and welcome us with baked goods. That's how we first met Betty and Syd Phillips—with pie. They were our next-door neighbors. An older couple, they were already grandparents. Syd was tall and bald with silver glasses, gray teeth, and a warm smile. Betty had short, curly auburn hair and always wore coppery lipstick and floral clothing. She had a hip problem, so she walked with a slow limp.

Betty and Syd came to all my plays and chorus concerts, always remembered my birthday, knew who my best friends were and what my favorite kind of pizza was. They were a part of our family. Syd took care of our plants whenever we were away, and we did the same for them. Betty invited my mom to her church's potlucks, where Mom brought deep-fried egg rolls or pot stickers, which the church ladies devoured. I remember how Betty flagged me down when I was walking home from the bus stop just to tell me how delicious they were and how lucky I was to have a mom who was such a good cook.

Betty and Syd loved children. Their own grandchildren lived far away, so Betty often invited my little sister, E, and me over to her house to bake cookies and other treats. Usually, there would be one or two other little girls from church there too. Betty would smile as we licked batter off spoons or pressed cookie cutters into dough and held up the cut-out shapes to show her. We always made a huge mess that left Betty happy.

Syd had a boat. On summer weekends, he took E and me and one or two other church kids out on the Chesapeake Bay. We waved goodbye to our parents as Betty and Syd loaded us into their car for the drive. Being out on the bay was exhilarating! We giggled and screamed in our swimsuits and life jackets whenever Syd made the boat go fast. But if he slowed down, we immediately demanded he go faster, squealing all over again. The cold breeze felt nice on our faces. Clearing our eyes and invigorating our bodies. For lunch, we had homemade sandwiches, Utz potato chips, and juice boxes that Betty packed in a red Igloo cooler. There was something about eating on a boat that made those soft cold-cut sandwiches taste really good. When we were closer to shore, Syd stopped the boat so we could jump off and swim. It wasn't deep, so you could stand up and feel the cold mud between your toes like silk. We scooped it up, putting it on our arms and faces, pretending we were glamorous women in mud masks at a spa. "The minerals are good for your skin," we said to each other, nodding, even though we had no idea if that was true.

I met my biological grandparents only a handful of times. They lived across the world and were unable to travel often. They didn't speak much English and I spoke very little Mandarin, and the language gap made it hard to share things with them. So, in many ways, Betty and Syd were my surrogate grandparents.

As my little sister and I became teenagers, we lost interest in baking and boat rides. Then I went to college, and my parents got divorced and Dad moved out of the house. After the divorce, things were different. My mom didn't hang out with Betty and Syd as much because it was different without the kids. Betty got hip-replacement surgery and was laid up for a while. I think Syd had cancer.

I started dating a much older guy, a quick and savvy New Yorker named Aaron. He was a tall Jewish guy who smoked cigarettes and breathed sarcasm. When Aaron first visited my hometown, he couldn't believe how many churches there were. He called anyone who was Christian a Catholic, which was strange to me because I'd grown up around a lot of Christians, but very few Catholics. Betty and Syd were Presbyterians. My best friend went to a Methodist church. A lot of kids I went to school with attended West End Assembly of God.

When Betty and Syd found out I'd brought my boyfriend

back home to visit, they wanted to meet him. So I took Aaron next door. They were so happy to see us. Betty made sugar-free zucchini cake—she'd heard I was dieting at the time—which she sliced and put on blue-and-white plates for us. We sat down on the wicker furniture in their carpeted sunroom and caught up. They asked questions about my life. Asked my boyfriend about New York. I said dumb, braggy stuff, trying to be cool. I wanted to prove I'd outgrown my roots and that I was *fine* after my parents' divorce. *Great*, even. That I was a cool city girl with an older boyfriend. But as obnoxious as I was, they thought every answer I gave them was just wonderful. They shared their love so freely.

That was the last time I ever saw them.

A couple years later, Syd passed away. Betty followed shortly thereafter. I didn't know about their funerals until after they happened. My mom cried when she told me. My chest felt hollow, like the air when it's cold and raining. I thought about Betty's azaleas in that cold rain. Syd's boat and the gray sky over the Chesapeake Bay.

That final time I saw Betty and Syd, when I took Aaron to meet them, when they made me zucchini cake and loved me even when I'd been so obnoxious, I remember feeling proud that they were my neighbors. Almost like I was show-ing them off. I thought my boyfriend would be impressed by their kindness. But the second we left their house, he started complaining.

"Jesus Christ," he said. "I've never heard anyone talk so slow. It was killing me. How the fuck does someone talk that slow?" He laughed. I felt a twinge in my chest. Suddenly, I wasn't proud of being a city girl anymore. Upset, I picked a fight with him—babbling nonsense, unable to find a point to anything I was saying because I didn't know who I was anymore, and I didn't know who I wanted to be. I had come home to Virginia and my house had been different because of the divorce, but my next-door neighbors had been the same wonderful people, and suddenly I was sobbing and couldn't stop. My boyfriend was baffled by the tears, which kept pouring out of me.

"That's just how people talk here," I kept crying to him, over and over again. "That's just how we talk."

Making a Scene

New York City could make you feel invincible, like any shit you were given rolled right back to the shit giver, and the same thing happened with love. The love that pulsed through the city was built on aggression: I give it to you, because I know you can take it. Because *we're both here*. Ever since I was a kid, I wanted to live in New York. Movies about the city had a grit that felt honest, earned. New Yorkers were unfazed. They didn't participate in bullshit. They had dry, sarcastic senses of humor. Their facial expressions were neutral and unaffected. Even the way they walked felt gritty: hard, brisk, and with purpose. I remember once, after stepping out of the subway car, I paused briefly outside the doors to locate the stairs. "You have to keep moving," someone scolded me. "You can't just *stop*." My face burned; I was ashamed for revealing myself as a tourist. From then on, I pretended to know where I was going even when I didn't. I thought that was how I'd finally earn the badge I'd longed for—the badge of belonging to New York City.

But at twenty-two, I didn't really belong yet. I was only pretending to belong. So when Ty asked me out on a date, it felt like I had been invited to the popular kids' table. He was thirty-six and he was a real New Yorker. We met at a dive bar on the Upper West Side. We were both there for different friends' birthdays that happened to be on the same day. Once our separate groups realized the shared birthday, we began mingling. Ty was tall and broad-shouldered. He had the kind of skin where you could tell he probably had freckles on his shoulders. He was with a group of guys his age. They talked about the Yankees vs. the Mets, the snobbery of Brooklynites, a game called credit card roulette. They were so New York.

I wasn't all that attracted to him, but I was excited about the date because I thought it somehow proved I was cool. Not only because he was a real New Yorker but also because back then, I thought dating an older guy distinguished me. That it made me more evolved than other twenty-two-year-olds and also better than women his own age because my youth made me prettier than them (an obnoxious sentiment that would bite me back in the ass years later).

Ty was wonderful on that first date. Held the door open for me, pulled out my chair. He steered and maintained good conversation about substantial topics. We skipped small talk and shared our thoughts on art and culture. He worked some kind of generic nine-to-five job but was an aspiring novelist. I considered myself an aspiring artist as well, and we impressed each other by declaring our dreams and pitying the mundanity of other people's lives. He loved sci-fi and fantasy novels, explained to me how deep and symbolic they could be. I feigned enthusiasm and interest to make him feel good about himself. As we talked, his eye contact felt like a wave of heat. It overwhelmed me.

After dinner, we kissed on the sidewalk, he put me in a cab, and I floated home. He texted me for the next few days, and we made plans to see each other again soon.

For our second date, we had dinner at a restaurant near his place, and after dinner, he said he had a gift for me. Could I come upstairs so he could give it to me? I felt a twinge of warning in my gut, but I ignored it—he didn't *look* threatening or shady in any way, and if you had been there, you would have agreed. Plus, I didn't want to insult his friendly invitation by making him think I perceived a threat. I mean, he was giving me a gift for gosh sake. So, I went upstairs. It's okay; he *did* have an actual gift. It was in a box about the size of a throw pillow, beautifully wrapped in brown paper and a red silk ribbon. He asked me not to open it until I got home. It was a sweet gesture, and I kissed him to say thanks.

The kissing escalated to some fooling around. I let him take some of my clothes off and I let myself be touched. He felt me between my legs, and I shyly pushed him away, but he could feel my arousal. He smiled and got a condom from his nightstand. He took off his pants and started putting the condom on—an obvious signal for sex—which I did *not* want. So I said, "Oh gosh, I'm sorry, I'm not ready to have sex with you."

I said it clearly. It is a thing I've always said when I don't want to have sex. I say it in a very specific way: I blush, embarrassed, and look up at the dude like a goddamn damsel—*allowing* him to be the "hero who takes care of me." (Ugh. I know. It's so lame, but it's also true to my feelings. Even after many years of therapy, I *am still* always genuinely self-conscious/apologetic about my body the first time I'm naked with someone.)

But as I blushed and got shy and *apologized* (ugh) for not being ready to have sex, he merely smiled, as if he knew better, as if my vagina's wetness was more telling than the words coming out of my mouth. He gently got on top of me and held my face in his hands. He kissed my lips, my forehead, and looked into my eyes. He was being so tender. I repeated, as seriously as I could, "Really, I'm not ready for sex," my face flushing. He smiled at me again like I was a baby kitten, held me close, kissed me, gently moved my legs apart, and then he . . . did it anyway.

I didn't fight back.

I just . . . gave up.

———

There are a few reasons.

Back then I had idealistic and romantic notions of sex. Sex always had to be meaningful, special, with someone I loved. And I *had* to keep my "number" low. I'd had only two sexual partners in my life, both of them loving, committed, long-term relationships. I was proud of that. My number was two and that's how I wanted it to stay for a while. But he had already penetrated me and that counted as sex. So it was too late for that. In that moment, the increase of my number was actually more upsetting than what he was doing. I had wanted it to be two! I liked it being two! I gave up because now it was too late.

In movies, rape scenes are often dramatic and violent. In those early New York days when I was trying hard to be blasé and cool, it was embarrassing to have big feelings or reactions. Even in this moment I wanted to be the cool girl. Cool girls didn't freak out. Especially when he was being so sweet and tender. Plus . . . he wasn't violent. He just didn't listen to me or didn't believe me—a feeling I knew well. And, while he was being tender *now*, if I fought him there was a risk that he could become angry or violent. Could I really fight someone twice my size and a decade older than me? In *his* apartment? Or what if he got mad at me? Called me crazy? Laughed and said, "Calm down, drama queen! I was just joking. Who do you think you are? I didn't even *want* to have sex with you, haha, *you really think you're all that hot*?" Then he'd get to be the cool guy, and I'd become the conceited girl who thought she was *all that hot*. I was already so embarrassed. Of my body, my arousal, my unacknowledged plea. So even though he and I were the only two people in the room, I didn't fight back because I didn't want to *make a scene.*

And since he was wearing a condom, I rationalized that it wasn't *that* bad.

It shames and confuses me even today to admit this part: I had an orgasm quickly, something that rarely happens the first time I have sex with someone. It remains the strangest orgasm I've ever had. The only way I can describe it is to say that it's like if you were having knee surgery and you had local anesthesia on your knee, so it was numb, but you could still feel the doctor operating—the taps of metal instruments, the pulling and movements of ligament and bone. You felt that, so you knew the surgery was happening, but you didn't feel the actual sting of the pain because of the anesthesia. Substitute "pain" with "pleasure" and it was like that. Like I had been anesthetized from the pleasure of an orgasm, but I still knew it was happening. I hate that it happened.

But I didn't give him any indication that I had orgasmed, and he didn't seem to care. He finished. He kissed me on the forehead again. Held me close. Cuddled me and nuzzled my ear. I tried to act normal. Pretended to be happy and content. Giggled to hide my fear and discomfort. He wanted me to stay over. I mumbled an excuse about needing to get back to my apartment for my skin care regime. I said "sorry" a million times.

He helped me get dressed and then handed me the gift box. He kissed me, said he couldn't wait to see me again. I took the box and kissed him back. "Thank you," I said. The sudden detachment I felt almost resembled . . . boredom. I wasn't even upset. I just felt . . . weird. Maybe because there had been no physical force; maybe because I had pretended that everything was cool afterward. But I didn't feel attacked or assaulted or coerced and I certainly didn't feel raped. Strange as it sounds, the word "rape" didn't even occur to me. *He just didn't listen to me*, I thought.

After promising to text him when I was home safe, I walked out of his apartment and down to the sidewalk. Found the subway station. Walked down the dirty stairs and stood on the platform. It was night and it was quiet in the tunnel. The train came. I got on, sat down with the unopened gift box in my lap. The subway car was one of those newer cars, with automated announcements, smooth gray-blue seats. I rode the train up to my apartment on 147th Street. I told myself I was tired even though I wasn't.

When I got home, I left the gift box on the kitchen table, unopened, and went to bed.

The next morning, my roommate asked about the box. "Oh," I said. "I forgot about that." She wanted to know what it was, so we opened it. Don't worry, it wasn't a severed head or dildo or anything like that. The box was filled with red rose petals. Nestled in the rose petals was a twenty-page manuscript of a short story he had written. It was called "The Beating Heart of the Forest." The pages smelled fresh. They were carefully bound in gold silk cord. I opened it up to the first page and read: "'If you travel beyond the purple hills of Aviandella, through the mists of the fertile valley, into the depths of the dark and enchanted woods . . . you will find it. You will find *her*. The beautiful Princess Warrior Constance Wu.'"

I kid you not.

After only our second date, he'd given me an original twenty-page medieval fantasy in which I was the central character.

A fantasy he'd written after one date.

Now, I know he could have pre-written it and plugged any girl's name into that story—I've heard that theory from dudes who want to make sure I know that I'm probably not *that* big of a deal. Thanks, guys. Don't you worry, I've heard that theory a lot! (And only ever from guys.) And I acknowledge that possibility . . . but you're missing the point. I'm mentioning the short story not to brag but to demonstrate that this story, original or not, was a gesture of romance, not malice. To show you that in his mind, he was a *nice* guy.

There was a part where Princess Warrior Constance Wu picks ripe berries from a bush in the forest and carries them in her white apron, staining it red with sticky, sweet juice. She rides a silver unicorn. There was a prince (his namesake) who rescues her from I forget what. In the end, two magical stones fall out of a tree into her (my) lap. The stones that legend called the beating heart of the forest. The last words of the short story?—"The wind whispered: *I was meant to find you.*"

Beneath the story, hidden in the rose petals, was an ornately etched pewter box. In the box was a pair of pearl earrings.

I looked at my roommate. What the . . . ?! "Are the pearls a symbol of his balls?" I joked. We both burst out laughing. The laughter was a relief. It was good to feel something.

"Have you even had sex with him?" she asked.

"Oh my God, no!" I lied. "This guy is crazy. He wrote this thing, and we hadn't even had sex!" This felt true, because technically he HAD written it and wrapped it up in a rose-petaled box before I came up to his apartment.

"Crazy!!!" we both said. It felt good to call *him* crazy. Like a type of power.

———————

After a while, that lie *became* true. I let the denial become the truth. My number went back down to two; it had never been up. The short story was such an outrageous thing, it overwhelmed everything else with its craziness. The narrative of that night became about the Princess Warrior story, not the sex. For weeks afterward he kept texting and calling. I didn't respond. Instead, I'd show my roommate his texts, laughing hard. "OMG. What a weirdo, right? Crazy!"

I kept the story in my file box, sandwiched somewhere

between copies of my parents' wills and my birth certificate, brandishing it whenever I told the anecdote to amused friends. I don't keep a lot of stuff, even meaningful stuff (I'm the opposite of a pack rat), but I told myself I was keeping it because it was so outrageous. But as I acquired more anecdotes over time, I stopped telling the story. There were new stories, and I forgot it even happened.

I dated other people, fell in love, went through heartbreak, moved across the country. I started to find success in my acting career—giving me a front-row seat to Hollywood's latent sexism and misogyny. I educated myself on rape culture and the unconscious ways "innocent" men unknowingly perpetuate it—how they let certain types of humor among their male friends slide, the way they make it about themselves (*not all men, definitely not me!* they cry).

In the past, I'd often played along with misogynist jokes; I liked being the cool girl who could laugh *with* the boys. It was an attitude that provided safety in places where I felt outnumbered. But as my profile started to rise, that kind of stuff started to piss me off. When my work in television gave me a public platform, I used it to advocate for equality, pointing out systemic gender biases, and calling for public acknowledgement of and ending to rape culture. Hearing rape survivors' stories didn't seem to trigger me. . . . It pissed me off in a way that I thought was activism. I'd hold their hands and listen. "One in five women experiences sexual assault. It's not your fault," I'd tell them. "You are not alone."

All the while thinking how fortunate it was that *I* had never been raped.

And then one day, out of the blue, more than ten years later, it all came back to me. I was on a plane from Singapore, where I had finished filming *Crazy Rich Asians*. I'd just woken up from a nap when the realization hit me like a flood. Ty raped me. He raped me, and I hadn't done anything about it. A strange sound involuntarily croaked out of my throat, almost a squawk—like an ocean bird with a large gullet, weeping . . . if birds could weep. Embarrassed, I hoped no one on the plane heard me. My heart was pounding. For a split second, I panicked. But then I talked myself out of the panic:

Oh. Oh my gosh. Oh. Well. Huh.

I guess that was . . .

I mean, I know it was.

But it feels weird to call it that.

It's also weird that I forgot.

But I'm honestly fine. I don't feel traumatized.

Oh, and he was trying to be a nice guy. He kissed my forehead and held me close.

I'm fine.

I couldn't call it "rape." Like, I couldn't even say the *word*. It felt way too dramatic and out of control for something that had been so . . . quiet.

I did talk about it with my therapist. She said it *was* rape and that the lack of violence didn't change that. She called it a trauma, a designation that felt wrong at times, convenient at others, and sometimes made me cry surprise tears. But what was most mysterious to me, what I couldn't fucking get over, was *how could I have forgotten?* I was *angry* at myself for forgetting, angrier than I was at *him* for raping me. And why had it suddenly come up out of the blue? More than ten years later?

My therapist told me how the mind can repress traumatic experiences—denial can be a survival tactic. But if it was so traumatic that it merited repression, then why did it come back at all? Why couldn't I have forgotten it forever? I couldn't figure it out. So instead of asking myself *why now?* I began to ask *why not before?*

What would have happened if I had remembered it sooner? If I had realized it was rape back when it happened, I could have reported it . . . but who would have believed me? After I had orgasmed, cuddled with him, pretended I was happy, accepted his gift, kissed him good night, even texted him *home safe, thank you.* He had text receipts and all I had was my voice saying I'm *not ready.* I hadn't, like, recorded it! Who would have believed me?

If the memory had resurfaced right when I became famous and my activism was finding its voice, I could have utilized it as a courageous confession to reinforce my political stance. But then I likely would have lied about the orgasm to simplify the story and protect myself from criticism.

Instead, the memory came back after I'd just finished a movie that would go on to be a huge success. I had money in the bank, I'd paid off all my debts, I had a steady TV job I was returning home to. I'd spoken at colleges and on panels where people came to hear me and actually listened to what I said. I think that's why the memory decided to resurface then. Because it was finally safe. I was financially and professionally secure. I'd reached a place in my life where people actually listened to me. That's when it all came flooding back: The way he cooed at me. The excited, greedy look on his face as he unwrapped the condom. Me repeating, *I'm not ready. I'm not ready.* Feeling small. The way his chest hair was thick and dry, like warm, loose moss. The dirty white kitchen cabinets in his studio apartment.

But still, it was all in my memory. There wasn't any physical proof so it didn't feel real.

Then, I remembered the short story.

It was a quiet summer day when I went upstairs to where I kept my files—in one of those big accordion file boxes. Because everything had become digital, I hadn't pulled it out in a long time. It was dusty, the out-facing side of the box faded several shades lighter than the rest. I sat on the floor of my den and opened it. The house felt quieter than usual, only the sound of my fingers skimming the files, a few cars on the street outside. And there it was. "The Beating Heart of the Forest." My heart sank and I simultaneously felt a helpless anger rising as I pulled it out. The paper was so stiff it made a crackling sound. The bold ink on the page, the black lines of the letters, so clear. For some reason, I couldn't believe the ink was still so crisp. It seemed impossible. As though, after so many years, I had expected the ink to disintegrate into the earth like compost. As if, like my mind had done with my memory, it could just fade away.

Then I remembered the phone call.

A few months after the night Ty raped me, I was walking to Banana Republic to return a "business look" I had bought and worn for a quick commercial audition when my cell phone rang. It was an anonymous number. I picked it up.

"Hi! It's Ty!"

I froze.

"I miss you!" he said, that familiar warmth in his voice. He picked up right where we had left off, as though months without communication hadn't passed. He was sweet, enthusiastic, and so glad I'd answered the phone. (Side note: one benefit of this experience is that it killed my curiosity about unknown callers.)

Panicked, I was nice back to him and said, "I'm running into an audition right now so could I call you later?"

He said sure.

———————

I never called him back. But I knew I didn't want to hear from him again. So I emailed: "I'm sorry about the lack of contact. You're great, but I just don't want to date you. I'm sorry."

I think he must have felt hurt and rejected, but instead of being sad that a girl didn't like him, he turned to anger. *He made a scene, calling me a heartless bitch, an ugly whore who would never get anywhere in life. He accused me of using him. He demanded I return the story and the earrings. I replied that I would, apologizing. But I never made it to the post office. I don't remember what happened to the earrings. That was the last I ever heard from him.

By now, I imagine he's married to an adoring wife who'd be shocked by my account, insisting *as someone who knows him, I know he'd never do something like that. He is not that kind of person.* As if the way someone treats you personally is the way they treat everyone.

Ty would probably be shocked too. Genuinely baffled. I can see that.

Whenever I hear a high-profile man defending himself against a sexual harassment claim, I often see how baffled he is. Blindsided. How he thought it was consensual. How, like Ty, he thought he was the *good* guy. The guy who made love to me tenderly and wanted to see me again and bought me nice jewelry and wrote me an entire love story. I can hear his earnest refusal in my head: "I have the text messages where she even *thanked* me for a nice night! She cuddled with me afterward! Then *she* ghosted *me*. . . . Then she dumped me over email when she promised she'd call! She's a thief too, because she never returned the pearl earrings or the story like she promised. And now she's calling *me* a rapist? In what world is this even plausible?"

I wonder if our culture tends to sympathize with accused men because their bafflement over the accusation is often so genuine. When men don't listen well, they might mistake the ways a woman covers her fear (giggles, silence) for consent. So for him, it's very clear cut. Whereas the woman? Her claim is filled with shame and guilt and regret over things she didn't say or do in the moment, for fear of making a scene. It's easier to side with the guy, whose feelings around it are less . . . complicated. To see him as a regular guy who made a mistake. To forgive him. That old Bible scripture *Forgive them, for they know not what they do.*

But instead of forgiving those who know not what they do, I think we ought to just tell 'em what they did. To give them the truth. I give it to you, because you should know how to take it. Because *we're both here.*

I did not consent to sex. Maybe it wasn't violent, but it was rape. Period.

Some people might say that I should have fought back against Ty. But if I could go back in time, I wouldn't even change how I reacted that night. Because when I think about the girl I was back then, I understand what she was going through, why she didn't fight back. She wasn't yet ready to bear the insults and derision that follow when women make scenes. And I wouldn't make her to do something before she was ready.

The only thing I'd change is that I wish I had told my roommate about what happened, instead of laughing about the rose petal box and short story. Not so she'd make me report it or anything, but so she could have held my hand. So she could have listened to me.

Playing Miranda in *The Tempest*

Little Cassandra

In scene-study classes at drama school, my acting teachers always assigned me ingenue roles: Juliet in *Romeo and Juliet*, Muriel in *Ah, Wilderness!*, Nina in *The Seagull*, Laura in *The Glass Menagerie*. When I ventured to ask them for more complex leading-lady-type assignments, I was shut down. They just couldn't see it. And sure, I was petite and wore girly clothing—but that was all on the outside. Inside, I knew there was more. But rather than letting me *try*, they insisted I embrace my "type." "Ingenue roles have a vulnerability and innocence that takes a lot of skill and courage," one teacher told me. "You're just scared of it! You have to dig deep. Face your fears. The hardest person to play—is your true self."

She had a point.

But how did she know who my true self was?

So when our acting company was assigned the *Oresteia* during our junior year, I was excited. Greek plays are enormous and raw and very, very challenging. I wanted to play Cassandra—the tragic seer. When she spurns Apollo's sexual advances, he bestows her with the ability of foresight coupled with the curse of disbelief—while she will be able to see the future, no one will ever believe her. In the Ted Hughes translation that we'd be performing, Cassandra closes the first act of the play with a fifteen-page speech. It's bloody and brutal and fucking awesome. Murder and savagery and pain, pain, pain.

The *Oresteia* was our Spring Show, which meant we *auditioned* for our roles. Casting assignments were often a foregone conclusion (we had "types," remember?), but we still went through the audition process. That meant I had a chance!

Hugo Kelly, a veteran stage director, would direct the play. He was a legend at our school. He'd won awards and had worked with Sandy Meisner, which was so rad. One day in an attempt to kiss up, my fellow company members Cynthia and Gretchen and I were talking to Hugo in the hall, gushing about our excitement for the *Oresteia*.

"It's going to be wonderful," Hugo said, beaming at Cynthia and Gretchen. "The women's roles are so great and strong." Then he looked at me with an expression of pity and apology and said, "I just don't know what we're going to do with the younger, little actors."

Then he petted me on the head like a puppy.

Okay, he didn't actually pet me on the head. But that's what it felt like.

I was the same age as everyone else in my company. And though I looked young, I was the same height as at least three other girls, including Gretchen. *The younger, little actors?* What he really meant was that he didn't know what he was going to do with *me*. Little me.

Feeling humiliated and helpless, I ran to the bathroom and cried. Fantasized about every comeback I could have said to Hugo in the moment—*Oh yeah? I'll show you little!* I imagined shouting as I kicked him in the balls, or *I only look little to you because you're SO fat!* Heart pounding as I played them out in my head, they were petty, childish insults that probably would have made me feel even worse. And anyway, the moment had passed. I'd have to find another way. That's when I decided, come hell or high water, I was going to win the part of Cassandra.

In the audition monologue, Cassandra arrives onstage bound in Apollo's chains—a symbol of her gift and her curse, they weigh her down. In the middle of the monologue, she sheds them. I wore a shawl to the audition as makeshift "chains," emotionally investing every fiber of my being into that shawl. When I walked into the audition room I was practically shaking with indignation and rage. Without a word, I took the center of the studio floor. Looked Hugo straight in the eyes and began:

> *Apollo! God of my guidance—*
> *You led me the whole long way*
> *Only to destroy me.*

She foresees the slaughter of children, cannibalism . . .
her own brutal murder. And it's too much—

> *This garb is ridiculous on me—*
> *This prophet's robe*
> *Wrapping me in my own dissolution,*
> *This staff, and these garlands—*
> *They bring me my own death—*
> *Get away from me.*

And then I shed Apollo's chains, my shawl dropping to
the floor. In that moment it was like I shed everything and
everyone who'd ever hurt me, underestimated me, humiliated me, made me feel small.

> *I curse you as you have cursed me.*
> *Trampling these, I feel some freedom*
> *From the curse of my life.*
> *. . .*
> *I've finished with tears.*
> *Finished with prophecy*
> *And the pitiless designs of fate.*

FUCKING BALLER SPEECH. Hard as FUCK to do.
When I started it, I had no idea how much would flow out
of me, but Cassandra came alive in my body—a roaring fire
of pain that pummeled through me. My emotions were enormous. Greek! Who was little now?

Hugo was stunned.

I got the part.

———————

I've always had to fight for my roles. In my career, casting directors often refused to see me for auditions, saying I was the wrong type, or that they couldn't picture me in the role. Undeterred, I'd find the audition sides myself, film myself, and email it to the casting director. Often refreshing the private viewing link over and over again, to check the view count. I rarely got parts that way, but I always tried. Even when it felt pathetic or embarrassing (which it almost always did). It's what I did for my role in the television pilot *Browsers*. I even did it after I was famous, for my role in *Hustlers*. I loved that script and that story. But my agents said that with my success, I didn't need to audition. That I ought to get a straight offer instead. After a few weeks went by without any word from the *Hustlers* team, I got antsy and decided to make my own homemade audition tape anyway. I emailed the link to my manager to forward to them, praying they'd watch it. For *Crazy Rich Asians*, I was told that my TV filming schedule conflicted with the dates. That there was just no way it could happen. But I didn't give up. I wrote an impassioned personal email to the director. I had the audacity to ask him to *change the filming dates for me.*

Though I usually take pride in my scrappiness, sometimes it feels unfair that I've had to fight so hard while other people just seem to be . . . blessed. You know those folks—

when they walk into a room, the air changes. They are the Golden Ones; you just *know* they're movie stars. You can't take your eyes off of them. Usually tall and striking, they have that "it" factor that I never had. They can screw up an audition and still get the part because the director feels that they just *are* the part. That there's no other choice.

That doesn't happen to me.

Hugo didn't think I could play Cassandra, and he wouldn't have cast me in the role if I'd been anything less than 100 percent in that audition. I'm little. I don't have the advantage of movie-star presence. This is not to say that the Golden Ones have no talent—they usually do; you *have* to have talent to succeed—it's just that they don't arrive wearing Apollo's chains. They can just arrive.

With Kit Williamson in Palm Springs, 2018

Poor Shark

D o you want to feel its size?"
Those were the exact words he hummed in my ear the first time we made out, drunk, outside a bar in Santa Monica. As ludicrous as that sounds—*its size*—it was sexy in the moment. I was already feeling *it* against my leg anyway, so I put my hand on it. Ample size. Very nice.

And that's how our fuckbuddy relationship began.

His name was Matt, and we met doing a staged reading of a play in New York. It had been an intense, unusual experience—the kind that made us war buddies before we were ever fuckbuddies. We'd gotten along great while working together, but never hooked up. As most acting projects go, we lost touch after a bit. And anyway, I'd moved to LA.

One day, he texted me out of the blue: Hey it's Matt from X—. I'm in LA, you live here now, right? Want to grab a drink? I should mention that he was super charming and super hot. So I said yes and that's how we ended up outside a bar in Santa Monica, in the shadows, standing on a patch of grass, his breath on my ear and my hand on "its size."

For the next three years, we saw each other on and off

whenever he was in LA. He always stayed with his childhood best friend, Chris, in the Pacific Palisades, so it never felt like he was using me for a place to stay. He was just using me for my body—but I was using his too. We called each other whenever we were lonely or horny. He often invited me to hang with his friends, but I never really wanted to, so I rarely did. I never invited him to hang with my friends. I didn't even tell most of my friends about him. When we were together, I preferred that it was just us.

We were responsive fuckbuddies. If I wanted him to come over, he'd leave his friends and hang with me all night. If he wanted me, I'd cancel my plans. We'd have sex, but then we'd talk all night and laugh and kiss and have sex again and talk more until we fell asleep. After a couple years of this, a natural level of comfort and affection began to develop.

One late night, we were both still wide-awake after sex, and hungry. So we went out for pie. We sat in a brown vinyl booth at an old late-night diner and ordered peach pie. Someone had left a newspaper in the booth. We opened it and did the crossword puzzle inside as we ate the pie. Comfortable enough with each other to not talk, we spent an hour in that old diner, our sides touching, just saying the words in the puzzle.

He never loved me. I know what love looks like—opening up from the center of the face, love melts the outer corners of a man's eyes, drooping them down toward the softest smile. It's a mixture of joy and sadness and need and wonder. I've had four men look at me like that and you absolutely know it when it happens. Matt never looked at me that way. That's how I knew it wasn't love.

The closest he ever came to looking at me like that was when he showed up at my door unannounced one night after a terrible audition. It was pouring outside. His hair was wet, his jacket was dripping, he was apologizing, his forlorn eyes curving downward with the rain but also upward to me, needy. I don't think I ever loved him, but that was maybe the only moment I felt something close to it.

We were never boyfriend-girlfriend; we lived on different coasts and neither of us wanted that, anyway. It was an unspoken agreement. But it got confusing sometimes. He treated me like a girlfriend. He believed in me, encouraged me. He taught me how to play guitar. He liked spooning after sex. He knew how to soothe me when I was upset. In his own way, he took care of me. When he was in New York and I just needed someone to talk to, he rarely picked up the phone when I called, but he'd always call me back within the hour, saying, "Hey, are you okay? I miss you."

When he was at a film festival in San Diego and he asked me to drive down, I did. I got in my little Prius and drove the two hours south, listening to albums by Beach House and Grizzly Bear and Real Estate that he'd burned on CDs for me. I thought I was driving to the film festival, but it turned out that the address he gave me was his family's house, where he was staying. He introduced me to his siblings and his parents, squeezing my shoulder. "This is Constance," he said, looking at me with affection. A strange warmth spread through my body and I felt myself turn bright red. I hadn't known I would be meeting his parents that day. That's what couples did, and we weren't a couple. It felt nice, but off.

Then we said goodbye to the fam, and he got us a hotel downtown. We had a disgustingly fat dinner, and some mediocre sex. But that was okay. We were comfortable enough that one session of mediocre sex didn't jeopardize anything. We could laugh about it. Afterward, we scrolled through the movies on demand, neither of us interested in any of them until we came across one that made us both turn to each other, exclaiming in unison, "*Never Let Me Go*!" It was that movie with Carey Mulligan and Keira Knightley based on the Kazuo Ishiguro book. We bought the movie and cuddled as we fell asleep watching it. The movie was okay, and we both slept well. It was a nice weekend.

We were fuckbuddies. But we were also buddies.

———————

And then one day, I was talking to my friend Kit when I casually mentioned our fuckbuddy relationship. After a few questions, Kit realized that he knew him and then he asked me if I knew that Matt had a girlfriend of fourteen years who he lived with in Park Slope.

I didn't.

Her name was June and he had been cheating on her with me the entire time. Matt never had any social media profiles (smart cheaters don't do social media), but his best friend,

Chris, did. I looked up Chris on Facebook and scanned his photos for someone named June. I found her. She was really pretty. Blond, blue-eyed, with the softest smile. She looked like someone who came from one of those families who *like* hanging out with each other. I clicked on her profile. She liked volleyball. She didn't wear makeup and her hair was usually in a ponytail. She was always smiling. She played the drums, and I saw some old pictures of her and Matt, when they were teenagers, in a band together. They really had been together for a long time.

I was stunned. His care had felt so sincere. How could a person lie so easily?

He was coming to LA the following week, so I waited to talk to him in person. When I confronted him about it, he broke down and admitted everything. "I don't know what's wrong with me, Constance. I'm awful. I've never been faithful to a woman. I can't help it. It's like I'm a shark, following a blood trail. I can't stop moving or I might die. June doesn't know anything. What's wrong with me? I'm a horrible person." He started to cry.

I ended up comforting *him*. It was a next-level manipulation that preyed on my sympathy. *Poor shark*, I thought.

But really, poor June. Matt was a shark, but June was a person. I bet he had squeezed her shoulder in front of his parents too. Made her feel loved, heard. Her face was so kind. How could Matt have done that to someone so kind? She looked like someone he should have treated better. She deserved better.

I gently told a weeping Matt that it was over between us, but he ought to either tell her or let her go. "You don't do that to people you love," I said. "You don't lie."

"I know," he said with a voice that *sounded* guilty, like someone moping and looking at his feet. But he was actually looking straight ahead, beyond me, through the window. I remember that detail because it was strange. His wandering eye line didn't fit the sorry tone in his voice.

After that conversation, I felt a lot of things—betrayal, depression, sympathy, fatigue—but also relief. I knew we were just fuckbuddies, but he had confused me when he did boyfriend-like things. *He introduced me to his parents, what could that mean?* Or *He came to my house in the rain, he needed me.* Even if he was a shark, it was a relief to finally know that he was a shark.

Several months later, he called me. "I'm in LA," he said.

"Matt . . ." I began to turn him down.

"I broke up with June."

I didn't know what to say. I was shocked. I was also kind of flattered.

"Can I see you?" he asked.

I had just been dumped by a guy and was in a low place, so I was glad for the attention and possibility. Maybe it could be love this time. I drove to Fairfax District, where he was staying with a different friend, Dan. I texted him when I got there, and he came out and sat in my car.

I soothed him as he talked about how hard it had been to break up with June. They were together so long; their families knew each other. He broke her heart. She moved out of their Park Slope apartment. He felt awful about it.

He told me about a new movie he just finished filming. It sounded like a big-deal movie, and he was one of the leads. So, while he was torn up about June, he was also happy about the movie. It was nice to talk to an attractive male with such ease, so in pathetic desperation I ventured . . .

"So . . . was this . . . did you break up with her for us? Could we be together?"

"Oh, babe . . . I don't know. I live in New York."

"Isn't . . . that why you broke up with her? For me?"

He was silent.

Humiliated, I started to cry.

"But I love you," I said, lying.

He didn't say anything.

"Don't you love me too?" I asked, still pathetic.

He paused.

"Babe . . . I got a lot of love for you, you know that," he said.

Ha. Even in the moment I thought those word gymnastics were funny. But I didn't laugh; I let it slide. Then he became sweet and gentle. He kissed me like the old Matt I knew before the truth had come out. He was romancing me all over again. We ended up having sex in the car.

Afterward, I felt light and happy. That's when I saw a familiar glazed panic rise in his eyes.

"I have to tell you something," he said. My heart dropped.

Her name was Megan. He had met her right after breaking up with June. They had been together for only three months, but a few weeks ago, when he finished filming that big movie, he had proposed to her. The fuckbuddy I had just fucked was engaged.

Okay. *That* was when I finally got angry. What a fucking asshole! He tried the sympathy route again—"I know, I don't know what's wrong with me, I'm like a shark . . ."

I shut him up and kicked him out of the car. It was over. I vowed to never contact him again.

———————

Four years later, I ran into him at a film festival. I'd had some success in my career at that point, and I was leaving a dinner to go to the closing-night party. As I stepped out of the restaurant toward my limo (what a look!) I heard "Constance!"

It was him. He looked great. But so did I (thank God).

He came over and hugged me. He congratulated me on all my success. Said how he always knew I would make it, how talented I was. Told me how beautiful I looked.

I was cordial but cold. "Thank you, that's so nice," I said. But then I motioned to my waiting limo, indicating that I had to go.

"Wait, are you going to the festival party later?" he asked, excited.

Not anymore, I'm not, I thought. But I told him maybe.

I didn't go to the party. He texted me all night. He was totally trying to fuck. I didn't respond to any of his messages. Zero. Instead, I befriended one of the festival interns. She was a local, so she took me to some fun bars instead of the party. We got drunk together and I told her the whole story. She became protective on my behalf and started dissing him every time he texted me. It felt good to have a friend that night.

The next day, my new friend drove me to the airport for my flight back to LA. And, whaddaya know . . . Matt was at my gate. When he saw me, his face brightened. I frowned, turned my back and found a seat as far away from him as I could. He walked over to me, stood in front of me. After a long moment, he sighed and said, "You hate me, don't you?"

I smiled a big, painful smile, cocked my head, and said, "Yeaaahhhh . . ." kind of shrugging as I did it.

He nodded, okay. And then he just stood there, seemed to be waiting for more.

After a moment, I asked, "How's married life?"

"It's . . . challenging," he said, a smug grin on his face.

Ugh. What a dick. I was definitely feeling its size now.

We boarded the same plane. I was in first class; he was in economy. As he passed me to get to his seat in coach, he chuckled and said, "Of course." And that was the end of our interaction.

———————

Until two years later. I was early for a doctor's appointment, so I went to my favorite café around the corner from the doctor's office. I ordered a coffee and some granola and yogurt and was just sitting down when he walked into the café. I didn't even recognize him at first. He had gotten so fat.

"I got fat," he said.

"Oh no, no, not at all, like . . ." I stammered, trying to recover.

"It's for a part I'm playing," he said.

"Oh," I said, relieved. "Cool."

I felt a little guilty in that moment. Our last interaction had been when he had asked me if I hated him, and I had shrugged and said yeah.

"Hey," he said finally. "It's okay. I get it. You were right."

We had known each other for more than ten years; used each other's bodies for so long. We had shared good stuff and bad stuff. But we were both still okay. A moment of silent understanding settled in the air as we both suddenly just let it go.

He sat down and we caught up, falling right back into our rhythm. This coffee shop was his favorite, he said. It was near his house. He had finally moved to LA! He asked why I was at the coffee shop. I told him about being early for my ophthalmologist's appointment, how I liked the granola they made there.

It was easy and fun. Talking about our friends, families, careers. And acting. Always talking about acting. We were both pretty obsessed with the craft. I had seen him play a small part in this TV show I really loved and told him that. He had seen and enjoyed my sitcom. We were proud of each other. I asked about his wife, sincerely. He was honest this time. Marriage *had* been really challenging. He and his wife really hadn't known each other when they had gotten engaged. There had been times when he had his bags packed and was headed out the door. But he stayed. "She and I are still learning each other," he said. I realized he possibly knew me better than he knew her. He'd certainly known me longer.

I ribbed him a little about how he had texted me that night of the film festival. "God, I'm such a dick sometimes!" he said, shaking his head and smiling. When I hadn't texted him back, it made him crazy. "I couldn't believe you didn't respond. I thought maybe you had changed your number or something."

"Ha. You would think that," I groaned, rolling my eyes, poking fun at his narcissism. We both laughed and the hatchet was fully buried. We talked until I had to go. We shared a genuine hug.

I walked out of that coffee shop happy to remember the good stuff. To know that, throughout all the lies and drama, our bond hadn't been false.

That was a while ago. We haven't called or texted each other since that day. But if we ever bump into each other again, I know it will be peaceful. And for that, I am glad.

With Lida Rose, 2013

Real Love

One day I just decided to do it. Since I was a little girl, I'd longed for this kind of love. I'd put it off for so long, afraid of the commitment. But now I was thirty-one and needed to stop chickening out. Heart pounding, I started testing the waters . . . looking at pictures online, imagining our first time meeting, preparing my bedroom. I was nervous and scared, but it was time: I was finally going to get a pet bunny rabbit.

The thing is, I already had so many bunnies—but none of them were real. I had bunny coffee mugs, paintings, jewelry. Bunny magnets, coffee table books, figurines. Bunny plates, salt and pepper shakers, calendars. Clothing with bunnies on it—dresses, socks, T-shirts . . . you name it. (In my defense, about 90 percent of these items were gifts.) When I was gifted a large chocolate bunny, I put it in the freezer and screamed at my boyfriend whenever he tried to eat it: DON'T EAT THE BUNNY. Was I on my way to becoming a crazy bunny lady? Nope. I was already there.

After some research, I decided on a Holland Lop. They're the ones with floppy ears. My friend Leah (who is a veterinarian) and I drove a couple hours east of LA to meet a lady who sold Holland Lops out of her garage. There were so many baby bunnies to choose from, but when I saw my bunny, I knew she was the one. Chestnut brown with a white belly, she was so tiny—the runt of her litter. As the runt, she was underdeveloped, and her ears were shorter than they were supposed to be—so they didn't flop. Instead, they helicoptered straight out to the sides. She seemed like she was the laziest of her litter, like I was (and still am) in *my* family. When I held her in my arms, she relaxed into a position that felt like a sigh. I'd found my bunny.

I named her Lida Rose, after a song in *The Music Man*.

Those first few months with Lida Rose were thrilling and terrifying. Every sneeze sent me on a paranoid internet frenzy to make sure she wasn't about to die. I went to the vet like seven times in four months. Bought her organic greens and changed her litter box every single day, sometimes twice. Spent hours staring at her with a dumb smile on my face. I took hundreds of pictures.

Getting to know her was gradual—lots of trial and error, behavioral observations. I learned that she loves to be pet on her forehead and nose, but not under her chin. Unlike other bunnies who huddle in their cardboard hidey-houses, Lida Rose likes to lie with the rear half of her body inside the hidey-house and her head outside of it, so she can see everything going on around her. She enjoys the feeling of being wedged. So I put two bricks on the floor, a few inches apart, parallel to each other. She wedges herself between the bricks and stretches out on her belly. It's her favorite spot. On hot days, I replace the bricks with two frozen water bottles. She wiggles herself between them and enjoys the cool of the frozen bottles, licking the condensation.

She stomps her rear foot when she hears a sound she doesn't like—and she hates the sound of clapping. The first few times she heard me play the acoustic guitar, she kept stomping her foot, but she doesn't anymore. Maybe she got used to it, or maybe I got better. Her food preferences are unique too—she likes cilantro but doesn't care for dill. She LOVES kale. She loves apples and bananas but is so-so on carrots. Oats are like crack for her, but she can't have too many. She's never been a biter. She's not defensive or aggressive like some bunnies, but she hates it when you "move her furniture around." For example, if she places an applewood stick or a toy in a certain spot, she doesn't want you to move it. The few times she's ever bitten me were when I "moved her furniture around." *I put it there for a reason*, she seemed to say. I learned that quickly. In her almost ten years of life, she has bitten three, *maybe* four, times total— all within the first year of having her. Now I know, if I want to reorganize her area, I need to distract her first with a treat or by petting her nose.

When you pet her, she relaxes into an almost hypnotic state. And if you stop petting her, she'll gently lick or nudge your hand to ask for more petting. When she was little, I'd pet her into relaxation mode, then stop and put my face right in front of hers. When she finally licked my nose, I rewarded her by continuing to pet her. That's how I taught her to kiss. Now, if I hold her up to my face, she automatically licks my nose. It's become a natural reflex for her, that kiss.

When she was about nine months old something strange started growing inside her left eye. It became inflamed, and when you looked very closely into her pupil, there was a white spiral blooming inside. It looked awful and I was frightened. I went to the vet, who sent me to a bunny ophthalmologist (there are animal ophthalmologists!). Lida Rose had *E. cuniculi*—a fungal infection that's very common in bunnies. When left untreated it often leads to rear-leg paralysis or an extreme head tilt. The doc said Lida Rose was lucky the *E. cuniculi* had affected only her one eye and not her legs or spine. A cataract had already started growing over her eye. They gave her a medicine that got rid of the fungus, but the vet said the cataract would likely thicken as her eye pressure increased. Lida Rose would probably go blind in that eye, they told me. She'd already lost a significant amount of vision. And while bunnies were fine having eyesight in only one eye, if her eye pressure severity increased, it would become painful for her. If it reached a certain pressure, she'd need eye removal surgery or it might rupture. But because it wasn't urgent yet, I decided not to do the surgery, hoping the eye pressure would stop increasing. Over the next year, as the cataract got bigger and bigger it made me feel helpless and upset. Like someone was hurting her, when she hadn't even done anything wrong.

I was scared of what would happen if I put her into surgery. And, selfishly, what she would look like with only one eye. It was a petty fear: *My perfect little bunny won't be so cute anymore*, I worried. But when the cataract got too big, I didn't want her to be in pain. I scheduled the surgery.

The vet's office was in Pasadena, in a specialty animal hospital that treated "exotics"—basically any pet that wasn't a cat or dog. I dropped Lida Rose off in the morning, and they told me to come back later in the afternoon. I was scared and restless and wanted to stay close, so I wandered around Pasadena alone for hours. It was a late weekday morning and the town felt quiet and uninhabited. I went into a Target store and looked at makeup and skin care products to distract myself.

When I picked her up, she was still drowsy from the anesthesia. Her sleepy face looked almost grumpy . . . and insane! Half her face was shaved down to the skin—which was pink with black patches, like a cow—and her eye socket was sewn shut. I started crying immediately. Not because I was scared or upset but because that ugliness in her half-shaved face made me love her so much more.

The surgery was a success. And once the fur grew back, it just looked like she was winking; I almost missed seeing her weird half-shaven look. I could tell by the way she moved and pranced that she was so much happier, glad the pain was gone. She had been blind in that eye for a while. Now it was just normal to her. Having one eye means you always know when she's looking at you. She likes to lay spread out on her side, her eyeless side against the wall, the other side keeping watch over her world.

She is my quiet, gentle companion. When I'm home, she roams freely in my house. She likes people, especially boys. If someone new comes over and sits on the floor, she turns and looks at them with her one eye for about ten seconds, then hops over, nudging them as if to say: *Okay, you can pet me now*. Sometimes, she'll put her front paws on their lap, craning her neck toward them to beg for more petting. To me, that's normal, but to most people, it's a delight to have a bunny come over to you and put her paws in your lap. And while she'll let anyone pet her, I'm the only person she lets pick up and hold her. Sometimes she likes it, sometimes she doesn't, but even after I've done something she hates—clipping her nails or giving her a butt bath—if I hold her to my face, she still kisses me.

I've flown on airplanes with her; I've snuck her into hotels. When I was filming *Fresh Off the Boat* for six years, I brought her with me to work almost every day. She loved being in my trailer. That way she wasn't alone all day. Neither was I. When I did the Sundance Labs in Utah, they offered a free flight. But because the airline didn't allow bunnies on board, I opted to drive myself all the way from Los Angeles to Utah, just so I could take her with me. Same thing when I shot a movie in Northern California. Instead of flying, I drove the eight hours up to Healdsburg with my bunny sprawled out in the backseat of my Prius, her one eye squinting at the sunlight dappling through the window.

Now that I've had her for nine years, I no longer panic at the slightest sneeze. I only change her litter box twice a week . . . once if I'm lazy (which is more often than I'd like to admit). Occasionally, like a sibling you take for granted, I'm even irritated by her.

But it's nice to come home and see her up on her hind legs, begging for a sprig of parsley or a cuddle. When I'm upset, petting her calms me down. And now that I have a real bunny, I don't feel like a crazy bunny lady anymore. I feel like a normal lady who has a bunny. All the excitement and drama of my bunny fever dream has faded. There's just too much poop to uphold the romance.

Domesticated bunnies live till around ten years old, and Lida Rose is fast approaching that. I've thought ahead to how life will be when she's gone. I guess I won't have to think about finding a bunny sitter every time I leave town. There will be no more litter boxes to clean. I won't have to sweat nervous buckets every time I clip her nails. But I'll miss those bunny kisses. The way she smells like sweet, clean hay. Watching her relax in the sunlight.

People often ask me, "Why do you love bunnies so much?" and I always want to ask back, why do we love anything? Listing reasons almost cheapens the love, in my opinion. I don't have *an explanation* for love. It's also kind of an insulting question. Like, no one ever says, "Why do you love your dog?" Why is it that love for certain kinds of animals is understood, but others require explanation? As if they're saying: *It's unusual! Hardly anybody loves bunnies, so please explain to me, how could a bunny possibly be as lovable as the love you give her?*

But everything and everyone is lovable to *someone*, even if it doesn't make sense from the outside. Love is not something earned through merit. It's something that happens with time. Even with the humans I've loved, that's what it often boils down to: time. All that stuff at the beginning of the relationship, the thrills and passion and attraction and drama . . . sure, that's wonderful, and I've called that love before. But real things don't have shortcuts. Those sublime whirlwind weeks often *feel* like love, but real love doesn't truly happen until the wind dies down and everything becomes a little plain. That takes time. So time, and everything that happens in it, is probably where you find real love. Forgiveness is somewhere in there too.

It's like my favorite passage in *The Velveteen Rabbit*.

"Real isn't how you are made," said the Skin Horse. "It's a thing that happens to you. When a child loves you for a long, long time, not just to play with, but REALLY loves you, then you become Real."

"Does it hurt?" asked the Rabbit.

"Sometimes," said the Skin Horse, for he was always truthful. "When you are Real you don't mind being hurt."

"Does it happen all at once, like being wound up," he asked, "or bit by bit?"

"It doesn't happen all at once," said the Skin Horse. "You become. It takes a long time. That's why it doesn't happen often to people who break easily, or have sharp edges, or who have to be carefully kept. Generally, by the time you are Real, most of your hair has been loved off, and your eyes drop out and you get loose in the joints and very shabby. But these things don't matter at all, because once you are Real you can't be ugly, except to people who don't understand."

Why had I been worried that removing her eye would make her less lovable? That's not how real love works. If someone stops loving you when your body changes, then they just don't understand real love.

You Do What I Say

Y ou do what I say," he said, shrugging. It was his catch-phrase for me, and he loved it. He said it real casually—not demanding or aggressive, but almost pleasant, like he was stating a fact:

"The sky is blue."

"Pizza is tasty."

"You do what I say."

M— was a Chinese American guy in his late thirties who wore fancy sneakers and a laid-back Hollywood affect—like he knew everybody, and everybody knew *him*. As one of the producers of my TV show, he was my boss and my greatest champion.

Fresh Off the Boat was my first-ever network TV pilot. My first screen test too. I was a theater actress who'd never done a network sitcom before and I'd screen-tested for the role against two beautiful, talented women with lots of television work under their belts. "Nobody wanted you. I had to fight for you," M— told me. And it was probably true! Studios want to hire names, not newbies. Though he'd occasionally praise my talent, more often he told me how hard it'd been to hire me. In an industry where I hadn't yet earned my stripes, I was grateful for his support.

He demanded a direct line to me at all times. "You wouldn't be here without me. You have to listen to me. I'm protecting you. Everything you think and do should go through me first," he said. Somehow he got my cell phone number before we'd even started filming. When my agents tried to negotiate business matters on my behalf, he intervened by calling me directly, annoyed that he hadn't known about it first. Scolding me until I felt guilty and apologized. "It's okay," he finally relented, "just make sure you do what I say next time." While I'd later learn that it was perfectly normal for an actor's agent and lawyer to handle business matters, back then I had no idea. M— made it seem like a betrayal. I didn't want to betray the one guy who'd gotten me the job! Better to just listen to him. I'd heard stories of actors fired for arbitrary reasons. Some were replaced after shooting an entire pilot—their roles recast and their scenes reshot. I didn't want that to happen to me. So when he said "you do what I say" . . . I did.

Like when he pressured me to fire my then agent to sign with his favorite agent, S—.

"But I love my agent," I said. "We've been through so much together; I can't do that to him. It would break my heart!"

"Don't be dumb," he said. "You have to strike while the iron is hot."

He had a point. I signed with S—. Though it had been

awful letting go of my old agent, I was flattered and excited to be represented by her.

"Good," he said. "I really pushed for you. This is a big deal. She loves you now."

By that point I was accustomed to his cues for gratitude, so I picked it right up. "Thank you so much, this is exciting!" I said, smiling brightly. And I *was* grateful, but I played it up for him. I knew I had to make an excessive show of gratitude to match his expectation for my behavior.

He patted me on the back, pleased with both of us. "Yeah. You do what I say."

As is typical with all big agencies, they also paired me with another, more junior agent who would handle my day-to-day affairs, while S— stepped in when it was time for the big guns. The junior agent they assigned me to was named P—. He was an attractive Asian American guy with sharp style and a slick attitude. He didn't walk down the hallways of the agency; he strolled. Smiling and careening like a college jock. Like M—, he seemed to enjoy playing the part of a Hollywood hotshot. I was glad to have him on my team— proud to have an Asian American person representing me. One day, he was leading me down the halls of the agency after a meeting. With one hand on my shoulder he lowered his voice and asked me, "You dating a white guy?"

I stammered a reply: "Um, yeah . . . he's white?"

He gave me a congratulatory nudge. "High five." He

grinned, subtly offering his other hand up in the air. "I'm dating a white girl too! Go us!"

Sigh.

I could tell he was trying to establish kinship. And even though I knew I was supposed to play along, I just . . . couldn't. It felt racist and insulting to my relationship—I didn't date my boyfriend because he was white! "Gross," I replied, disguising my disgust with a smile and half laugh. "I'm not high-fiving you for that, dude! Haha!" And I didn't.

Still grinning, he sighed and shook his head. "Relax," he said.

That agency was never a good fit. I told them I wanted to work with the director Ruben Östlund, after seeing his film *Force Majeure*. Instead, they tried to get me to audition for *Baywatch*. Not tryna shade *Baywatch* but anyone can agree that it is a totally different world from *Force Majeure*. The agency just didn't get me or hear me or both. I didn't have to stay with them, but M—? He was my boss for as long as I was on the show, and the show had me under contract for a long time.

Which was fine, at first . . . great, even! He really was my protector and I needed one. My friends were all theater nerds or indie film buffs, none of whom had experience with network television. M— became my only resource. When I lost myself, he brought me back down to earth. Kept me from saying and doing reactive things that would hurt my career. He took time to care for me.

As our relationship became more buddy-like, our conversations started bleeding over into my personal life. While my personal life was not an area that I needed his guidance in, he tried to offer insight there too. He told me the way he preferred my hair. "Guys like long hair." Told me I looked better in short skirts and should wear them more often "while you still can," he'd say with a smirk. He kept tabs on all areas of my life: what other acting jobs I was auditioning for, which publicist to choose, what I wore in interviews, what parties I should go to, who I needed to be friends with, what I did in my spare time. He asked to see pictures of my female friends and would tell me if he'd fuck them or not. He constantly questioned me about my dating life, past and present. At the time of the pilot filming, I was in an off phase of my on-again/off-again relationship and I was sensitive about it. But even when I told him I didn't want to talk about it, he was relentless, demanding to see pictures of this boyfriend. I finally showed him one. After seeing how handsome and fit he was, M— frowned. Later, he texted me that I needed to date pudgy guys like him. Guys who didn't work out because they were too busy producing big-time television.

Sometimes, he texted me late at night, requesting selfies. It made me feel uncomfortable and I didn't want to. So I made excuses like: Gah! Sorry I hate selfies, they make me feel so narcissistic! He thought that was stupid. "It's not a big deal," he told me later. "Lots of actresses send me selfies."

I didn't complain about his behavior because I didn't think I was upset about it. I liked him—he was easygoing, funny, and in the know. I'll admit that I sometimes even enjoyed it; it felt good to feel like part of the boys' club. So even when he got a bit power trip–y, I always did what he said. When he became controlling, I let him, rationalizing that he *did* know the industry better than I did. When he was downright offensive, I came up with tricks to play along without entirely compromising myself. I'd laugh and roll my eyes at his casual sexism, saying, "Ugh, you're such a duuuuude, haha" (a retort that always worked because he was vain about his masculinity), or "Haha, oh my God, you're such a dick"—a statement for which he'd reward me with a grin and a pat on the back (real friends can razz each other like that!).

The few times I was honest about my discomfort, he scoffed, "Relax, it's a joke." Or he listed all the female directors he'd hired as proof that he wasn't sexist. It was true—he *did* hire lots of female directors, and he always spoke to *them* with respect and professionalism. (His sexism seemed reserved for young Asian women who weren't in positions of power.) And when I thought about all our female directors, I felt guilty for not giving him more credit.

It was easier to play along. Besides, there was so much to be happy about! People were touting *Fresh Off the Boat* as a historic milestone for Asian American representation in

Hollywood. It had broken barriers, started necessary conversations, given us a platform, and created opportunities. We were all so proud of it. So what if he was a little sexist or controlling now and then? It was annoying but tolerable. When I considered everything he'd done for me and for the Asian American community, was I really going to give him shit? And because he was married with a kid, it never felt serious. It was just harmless fun, right? Then the basketball game happened.

THE SCENE: M PRESSURES CONSTANCE TO DO WHAT HE SAYS

Disclaimer: While the following phone call is written as a single incident, its dialogue is culled from a variety of similar spoken conversations. M— often pressured me to go to non-work-related events—a basketball game, a baseball game, a party, a dinner. I've combined them here into one conversation to demonstrate the various persuasive tactics M— often used.

INT. BEDROOM - DAY

Constance sits on the floor of her bedroom, feeding parsley to her pet rabbit. It's a rare moment of quiet and she smiles.

Her phone rings: M— calling.

She looks at it and sighs. Then, plastering on a chipper face—

> CONSTANCE

Hey, dude! Sup?

(Her practiced tone is familiar, like she's talking to an old buddy.)

> M—

(off-screen)

What you up to tonight?

> CONSTANCE

Oh, you know. Just petting my bunny!

> M—

No, you're not. You're coming to a Lakers game with me.

> CONSTANCE

. . . What?

> M—

I got great seats. Steven gave 'em to me. For us.

> CONSTANCE

Who's Steven?

> M—

You know, Steve!

CONSTANCE

. . . ?

M—

Steve-y boy. Steve-man. The Stevester. Even
Steven. Steve-o.

*(Constance holds back a sigh. She's used to his
name-dropping. It's a role he loves to play—where his
casualness makes him seem cool and in the know, and she's
supposed to play the neophyte to accentuate that. But right
now she's not playing the part; she genuinely doesn't know
who he's talking about.)*

CONSTANCE

Sorry . . . I don't know who you mean?

(M— chuckles.)

M—

Spielberg.** DUH.

*(**Side note: Not actually Spielberg, but another Hollywood
big-wig who I won't name.)*

CONSTANCE

Oh. Haha, right. I've never met him. I didn't
know you knew him.

                    M—

Yah. We got his seats. You and me. Lakers
game.

                CONSTANCE

Thanks for thinking of me, but to be honest,
I'm not really into basketball.

                    M—

Oh, come on!

                CONSTANCE

I'm not! It's, like, only exciting for the last
two minutes of the game! Everything else is
just a warm-up!

                    M—

But this is a Lakers game. Steve-o's seats.
You're not saying no.

                CONSTANCE

I am saying no, actually.

                    M—

You don't have any other plans tonight. You
spend too much time with that bunny. I'm
picking you up at six.

CONSTANCE

Ha. I'm really not into basketball. And you
don't know my address, haha.

M—

Yah I do. You work for me. I can just look it
up, babe. C'mon. It'll be fun.

*(Constance knows she isn't going to win this battle.
And even if she did, he'd be attitude-y with her about
it later.)*

CONSTANCE

Okay! But I'm only going for the snacks.

M—

Whatever you want.

CONSTANCE

Beer and hot dogs.

M—

All the hot dogs you want.

CONSTANCE

Haha! Sold!

*(She jokes and laughs. M— appreciates the good nature of
it all.)*

> M—
>
> Yeah! You do what I say! See you at six.
>
> Wear something cute!

After she hangs up the phone, Constance's smile fades. She sighs and goes to her closet.

EXT. CONSTANCE'S HOUSE - LATER

Constance exits her house wearing cutoff jean shorts and a plain cotton tank top.

M—'s convertible coupe purrs outside as he holds the passenger door open for Constance in a very gentlemanly manner.

> CONSTANCE
>
> Thanks!

(He smiles, closes the door for her, and strolls back around to the driver's side.)

INT. STAPLES CENTER - LAKERS GAME

The seats aren't courtside, but they're pretty good. Constance sits with a beer as she polishes off her second hot dog. She isn't paying attention to the game. M— also sips a beer and watches her eat. He seems annoyed that she isn't more excited by the game or grateful for the seats. He gives her a look as she scarfs down her hot dog.

M—

Are you okay?

CONSTANCE

What do you mean?

M—

You're, like . . . acting weird.

CONSTANCE

Oh, sorry, I just, well, remember I *did* tell you
how I wasn't into basketball.

(M— stares at her for a long beat, still annoyed.)

M—

Let me get you another beer.

(Constance puts on a fun, silly face.)

CONSTANCE

Yes! I *am* into beer! Beer me!

(M— relaxes, glad for the return of cheerfulness.

. . . Later

*Constance now feigns enthusiasm at the game. M—,
pleased, puts his hand on her bare thigh.)*

M—

Your skin is so smooth.

CONSTANCE

What are you . . . heh, what are you doing?

*(She swats his hand away in a nonthreatening, playful way.
M— grins and tightens his grip, moving his hand farther
up her inner thigh.)*

M—

Relax. It's a compliment.

*(Constance good-naturedly rolls her eyes at him,
chuckling.)*

CONSTANCE

Haha. Oh my God. You're such a dude.

(He grins and slides his hand up to graze her crotch.)

CONSTANCE

Dude. C'mon, stop. STOP!

*(It's a rare, unexpected moment of sternness from her.
M— removes his hand, his face suddenly bitter. He hunches
his back away from her to watch the basketball game. After
a long moment of punitive silence, M— turns to Constance
and lightly pulls at the flesh on her triceps.)*

A bemused smile on his face, he squeezes her upper arm fat
and jiggles it around.
Constance looks at him with a quizzical smile.)

CONSTANCE
What . . . um. What are you doing? You
weirdo, haha.

(He smiles and inspects her triceps a little more closely.
Then, shrugging—)

M—
Nothing.

(After a beat, he releases his grip. He smiles as he pats her
on the back. Then, in a gentle, fatherly tone, says—)

M—
No, you know what? It's good. It's good that
you have big arms. It means you're strong.
Strong women are great. Good for you.

(He pats her thigh reassuringly.)

EXT. STAPLES CENTER - LATER

They pass a Nike store on their way out of the stadium.

> ### M—
> You been in this store before?

> ### CONSTANCE
> No, but I mean, I've been in a Nike store?

> ### M—
> No, no, this one's different. Hold on, I'm
> gonna get you something. Watch this!

*(He takes her into the store. From outside the window
we see him order a personalized T-shirt for her. He directs
the store clerk on exactly which shirt and what he wants
it to say. After paying for it at the cashier, they come back
outside to wait for it to finish printing.)*

> ### M—
> Let's go grab a bite.

> ### CONSTANCE
> Gosh, sorry, I'm so full from all the hot dogs!

> ### M—
> Okay, we'll just get a drink, then.

> ### CONSTANCE
> Oh, sorry . . . I kinda need to go home to
> memorize my lines.

M—

Fine.

*(He goes back in the Nike store to wait for the shirt,
leaving her alone on the sidewalk.*

. . . Five minutes later

*Coming back out, he shoves the Nike bag into her chest.
Without looking at her, he begins walking toward the
parking garage. He pulls out his phone and starts texting
in silence.*
She jogs to catch up with him.)

CONSTANCE
Thanks for the shirt. It's really cool!

*(He shrugs, picking up his pace. Unsure of how to remedy
his irritation, she offers—)*

CONSTANCE
I can take an Uber if you want?

M—

No. It's fine. I'm taking you home.

*(He keeps walking several paces ahead of her. Still texting,
he beeps his car open, jumps in the driver's seat, and starts
the engine. Constance, struggling to catch up, barely gets in
the passenger door before he pulls away.)*

<u>INT. CAR - CONTINUOUS</u>

The radio is turned up loud, neither of them speaking. M—'s phone buzzes and he checks it. Then he lets out a big, contented sigh. Staring at the road, his face fixed in an expression that can only be described as disgruntled contentment, he gestures to his phone and bellows—

>   M—
> You know what the best thing about
> producing this show is? That I can
> fuck whatever aspiring Asian actress
> I want to.

(A beat. She ribs him, good-naturedly.)

>   CONSTANCE
> Haha, I would have thought that being
> able to make a groundbreaking TV show
> that people enjoy would be the best part
> of your job.

(He shrugs, a shit-eating grin on his face.)

>   M—
> Nah . . . just the fucking.

(It's an invitation back into the boys' club! Constance jumps at the opportunity to break the tension.)

CONSTANCE

Haha, oh my God, such a dude!

(He laughs and relaxes. Finally, a truce! Constance grins at him, playfully raising an eyebrow.)

CONSTANCE

What about your wife?

M—

(casual)

Eh. We have an arrangement.

(Constance can feel the hot air of his lie. She knows there's no "arrangement," because she knows he doesn't actually cheat on his wife. It's all talk. But she plays along, giving him his favorite insult/compliment—)

CONSTANCE

Oh my God. You're soooo Hollywood.

(M— looks pleased.)

Boy, I was getting good at this.

———————

Later, he asked me for a selfie wearing the shirt he bought me, preempting my usual refusals by saying that he paid for that shirt and needed to see me in it. I reluctantly sent him a very boring, casual picture of myself. The next day, he told me it wasn't sexy enough. "Selfies are supposed to be sexy. Guys like that," he said.

Aside from that basketball game, he never touched me inappropriately. To be honest, it didn't feel like a big deal at the time. I was fine. Happy, even! I was genuinely grateful for his support, and it made him feel good to protect me, too. It was a win-win situation where he was the helpful to my helpless. But to maintain that dynamic he needed me to be helpless. And for a while . . . I was.

Fresh Off the Boat was a mid-season show, which meant it premiered in the spring. Most new network sitcoms premiere in the fall, while they're in the midst of filming. That means they see reviews and ratings in something close to real time. While *FOTB*'s mid-season premiere was considered less prestigious, the upside was that we got to finish filming the entire season in a bubble, without the added pressure and anxiety of ratings and reviews. But for me, an unknown newbie, that wasn't an upside. Good reviews would have bolstered my job security. But I'd have to wait. Until our show premiered, my future with the show felt like a big unknown.

When the show finally premiered, it was a critical and commercial success. We got picked up for another season and I was thrilled! With all the acclaim and one season under my belt, I wasn't so helpless anymore. That's when I started getting tired. Tired of M—'s cues for excessive shows of gratitude, tired of the casual sexism, tired of him keeping tabs on all areas of my life. And also just plain *tired*. Like, physically. I was filming five days a week, twelve-plus-hour days (thirteen when you include lunch). My daily commute totaled three plus hours of driving in LA traffic. So that was sixteen hours by the time I got home. (Side note: This was before the production studio implemented their improved overtime rules.) If I wanted a decent night's sleep *and* a shower, I was left with maybe an hour or two to eat dinner or pick up my room. And on the weekends, I did press for the show. Photo shoots, podcasts, interviews, appearances. This is not a complaint, but simply a description of my hours at that time. It took a couple seasons of trial and error to figure out how to regulate my energy throughout the day to maintain this schedule and keep my endurance up. But for the first and second seasons? I turned to jelly beans, eating them by the handful whenever I got tired. The sugar pumped me up enough to get through the end of the shoot, and then I'd crash—feeling gross and drained as I drove home in my dirty, old Prius (who has time for a car wash?).

In hindsight, I should have asked for help. The income I made from the show provided me with the resources for it. But I'd only recently graduated from waiting tables, so the idea of hiring an assistant or asking for any kind of help seemed like an insane jump. I didn't even hire a cleaning person for my apartment until season 4 of the show. *Why pay someone to do something I can do myself?* I thought. Growing up, my family had never had a cleaning person; it seemed like an extravagant expense.

In my twenties and early thirties, therapy was the only "extravagance" I allowed myself. Therapy was my oasis—a chance to breathe and catch up with myself. I had a therapist who'd seen me regularly for more than ten years on a sliding scale. I looked forward to it every week. But once I started the show, my filming schedule didn't allow time for our sessions. Occasionally my therapist would make herself available for a weekend or late evening, but she had two kids and a baby to plan around, so I always felt guilty asking her. I guess I could have found a new therapist with more flexible hours, but I didn't want a new one. I trusted mine; she already knew all my stories. The prospect of retelling my life to another therapist seemed exhausting, and I was already so tired.

My body was tired from the long days. My bedroom was always a mess because I didn't have time to clean. My mind was tired from the anxieties of public exposure. My face was tired from trying to be who everyone wanted me to be. And without time for friends or therapy, my soul was drained.

That's when I started saying *no*.

First, it was *no* to putting up with M—'s jokes. While I remained professional, I stopped the fake laughter and permissive razzing. Stopped all the "Haha, omg, you're such a dude." M— felt the difference and it irritated him. "What's wrong with you?" he'd ask.

Next, I started to say *no* to all the extra stuff . . .

Like when M— asked me to do an unpaid promotional event for Panda Express over a weekend. I'd already gone above and beyond my contractual duties promoting the show. And I didn't want to do the Panda Express promotion because I'm generally not a proponent of fast food of *any* kind. Besides, our show had already received criticism for being a watered-down, Americanized version of its source material. Which made being a promotional tool for Panda Express feel . . . weird. I told M— as much, and he said I was being difficult and ridiculous. That everyone else was doing it and I needed to get the fuck over it. When I told him *no* again, he canceled the event, opting instead to have Panda Express cater one of our table reads—where he knew I'd be. "You don't have to eat it," he said, and snickered as people took photos of the cast and me with the food in the background.

Then, it was *no thank you* when the cast was invited to make an appearance at an Asian American film festival, out of town. When I passed on the event, weeks before the festival, the network wasn't bothered because it wasn't a big deal. But unbeknownst to me, M— had assured people that he could get me to come. *She does what I say.*

A few days before the event, M— came into my trailer after a long day of shooting and told me I had to go. I said no.

"Why? What do you have to do instead?"

I guess I could have made up an excuse, but I didn't want to lie. I wanted it to be okay for me to say no. "I just want a weekend to myself," I sighed.

He tried to bribe me, saying it would be like a vacation. "We'll cover your stay in a five-star hotel. Unlimited room service, your boyfriend can come, we'll get you a nice car with a driver. A professional hair-and-makeup team to glam you up!"

But I didn't want a fancy hotel or a glam team. It had been a long time since I'd had an entire weekend off and all I wanted to do was go home to the house I shared with my three roommates, sleep in, clean my room, laze around, and have the biggest decision of the weekend be what dive bar we went to.

"No," I repeated.

His face hardened with rage. He couldn't believe it. Couldn't believe I wouldn't *do what he said*. He lectured me that it was for my own good, that he was only trying to help me, that I was insulting the AAPI community if I didn't go. That everyone else was going and if I didn't it would make me look bad. That I was being difficult and it would hurt my career. That he was protecting my reputation and he could just as easily ruin it. (Privately, I wondered if I were a white actress, would I have been labeled "difficult" for not wanting to attend a film festival during my time off? It's not like I had a film in the festival.)

For a second, I considered changing my mind. I could have gone. It would have been a nice gesture, and I didn't have any schedule conflicts, so it wasn't a big deal. As I sat on the worn brown chenille love seat of my eighties-era trailer that night I worried that maybe he was right, maybe I was being difficult, maybe everyone would think I was an asshole, but it was late at night and I was tired of everyone telling me what to do and I was scared and lonely and nervous and felt pulled and pushed all over the place and I just wanted *one* fucking win. One battle that I could claim so I could feel like I had some semblance of control over my life. So I dug my heels in, face burning, and repeated: *no*. Even if it was assholery, at least I'd get to *choose* assholery.

That's when he started shouting. "This is a make-or-break moment for all of Asian American representation,* and you won't even do this one damn appearance?"

As his rage built, my heart started pounding and all my internal alarms screamed *danger!danger!danger!* but I persisted, "No."

He put his foot down. "You HAVE to," he said.

I put my foot down, harder. "No, I DON'T." A rush of hot blood surged through my body, flooding down to my toes and erupting back up through my heart and mouth into the wail of a petulant child—small and full of tears and feelings that I didn't have words for. "No. I won't go! I don't want to! You can't make me!"

He stormed out of my trailer, slamming the door.

Whatever it was we'd had was over.

For the remaining few years of the show, we didn't speak. But while his friendship with me died, his relationships with

---

*It wasn't.

everyone else blossomed. Because even with those lowest on the totem pole he displayed a gentle warmth and camaraderie that he'd switch off whenever I came around, making sure I felt the contrast. I'd come on set and see him laughing good-naturedly with a PA, and when I approached his vicinity, his smile would immediately fade as he lowered his voice and frowned. Then he'd share a knowing look with the PA as he steered them away to continue their conversation elsewhere. Away from me. No one knew why M— and I had stopped being friendly. The timing of it made me look horrible—like I was the diva who suddenly refused to speak to him once she became successful. He made sure I felt like an outcast on set.

Sometimes I tried to forget it. To be carefree like everyone else. But I felt like such a fake when I did that. The fakeness felt so bad that I started hating myself for my inability at happiness and I withdrew. It was a helpless feeling, knowing that it was too late for anything to change. Like I'd started out on the wrong foot, and too many steps had been taken since then to go back. I couldn't go back unless I told people what happened.

I made a feeble attempt at this around season 2, telling a couple of my costars and the activist father of one of the child actors. "M— sexually harassed me." The general response was sympathy followed by questions: "What did he do?" Ashamed, I'd meekly pout and say, "I don't want to talk about it. . . ." Scared that my story wasn't "bad enough" to merit my feelings. Because when I recounted the offenses in my head, they sounded so paltry that I felt stupid. Maybe I *was* crazy. How could my pain be valid when I didn't have a scar to show for it? No one else on the show had been treated this way. I had no physical wounds to point to, no known allies who shared the same experience. What was I supposed to say? That he complimented my smooth skin and shared harmless little jokes with me and pressured me to sign with one of the top agencies in Hollywood and touched me over my denim jean shorts? And did it even count if most of it happened when I was off the clock? I felt like a hot, engorged tomato in a microwave: already thin-skinned to begin with and then permeated all over by invisible toxic waves . . . ready to burst at any moment.

And then, even after I'd told a few people about M— sexually harassing me, I'd see those same people sharing affection with him. My child costar's activist dad introducing M— with generous praise on an AAPI advocacy panel. Or my actor costars talking shop with him about future projects or mutual industry friends. The ease of their interactions made me feel betrayed or not believed, or both. I'd retreat to my trailer and weep. What could I do? M— was the relaxed boss who had it all together. I was a dumb steaming tomato who couldn't even form sentences to describe my experience.

In hindsight, I realize I put my colleagues in an unfair position. What were they supposed to do? Out my story without my permission? Or suddenly chastise their boss for something that I'd refused to qualify? Possibly jeopardize the whole show and everyone's jobs? I couldn't blame them for not wanting that, especially when I was too chickenshit to even make an official complaint. And this was all before Harvey Weinstein. By the time the #MeToo movement came around, *FOTB* was already a few seasons in, and the show had been established as a positive milestone for Asian American representation. Did I really want to stain that?

So I never went to HR, never reported it. No one encouraged me to either.* I didn't want to be the dumb steaming tomato who cried microwave.

Another reason I never said anything was self-preservation— I was ashamed of some of my own poor behavior. See, I thought I'd "handled" all the fear and intimidation of that first year by swallowing it, or by playing along. But repressed feelings don't just disappear and they inevitably came out in other ways: paranoia, jealousy, isolation. The smallest slight produced a disproportionately large reaction.

---

*Of the few people I told, only one person ever encouraged me to report it. It was years later, post–Harvey Weinstein. At the CAA AMPLIFY event in Ojai, I confided to a woman who worked at the same studio as M—. She knew him and wasn't surprised. She urged me to report it to HR, but I refused, claiming that it would reignite painful memories that I didn't care to revisit. Undeterred, she tried convincing me again, saying that it was important that these things were documented, or else the cycle would never end. I became stubborn and defensive, continuing to refuse. Later, she tried a third time—she found my phone number through the AMPLIFY directory and called me to communicate the importance of an official report. "It's just an HR claim," she said. I kept shutting her down. I was too scared. Too worried my story wasn't "bad" enough. That no one would believe me. I wish I'd listened to her. She was right, of course. I should have reported it and I am sorry I gave her a hard time.

Uncharacteristic, illogical behavior followed. The feelings were so large that even when I knew better, I couldn't help myself. Like the time I got upset with my costar Randall when I was accidentally excluded from a radio interview we were supposed to do together. I accused him of taking the opportunity away from me. Of trying to steal the spotlight. But Randall wasn't like that. Ever. He hadn't known (his publicist's error) and he felt awful—apologizing profusely and calling his publicist immediately (in front of me!) to make sure it didn't happen again. But I remained upset, punished him for days by pouting every time he came near me. Looking back, I cringe at my childish behavior. He didn't deserve it and I'm still so sorry.

Another time, when a director seemed to favor Chelsey, who played my friend and neighbor on the show, I became cold to both of them—it was my petty way of punishing them when really, I was just jealous that they were able to enjoy themselves on set. Bitter about my own inability at finding happiness on set, I was trying to deny it to others. It was awful. I wouldn't have wanted to be friends with me either.

Or there was the time M— said I couldn't go to my best friend's wedding in Bogotá because of a table read. I'd had the dates previously approved and cleared by production, so I'd already booked my flight. Then they changed the date of the table read and it conflicted with the wedding. When M— insisted I cancel, claiming that it was mandatory, that it would make me look bad if I missed the table read, I texted him angrily, threatening to call the studio executives if they wouldn't let me go. He "protected" me by not letting me do that, saying he'd take care of it. In the end, I was able to go to the wedding (I'd later learn that missing one table read wasn't an unusual actor request).

And then there was my general newness to the TV industry. I didn't understand the terrain of the business yet, so I was wobbly. I didn't even know the terminology—what a "forced call" meant or what a "one-liner" was. I didn't have friends or relatives at this level in the industry, I had no context for standard practices. And because I was an adult, I felt stupid and embarrassed asking questions that even my child costars seemed to know the answers to.

Back in the days when I'd been a struggling waitress/ actress I'd been taken advantage of a lot. It's unfortunate that success was a precondition of basic human respect for an actress—but that was the reality I learned when I got a TV show. It was unsettling and confusing. I'd kept my head down and swallowed disrespect for so long, that when I finally received some semblance of respect, I clung to it like the only life raft in a sea of drowning rats. Paranoid or suspicious or both, I wasn't yet sure when something was a normal actress request or if I was being taken advantage of. And then I'd hear stories of white actors refusing to do things that M— said I *had* to do or else I was *ungrateful*. . . . I didn't know what to believe. Was it *really* ungrateful behavior? Or normal? Or was it only ungrateful in the context of an Asian woman's rare existence on the playing field? And even if it was the latter, didn't context matter? If I was so lucky as to be on that playing field, maybe I had to be perfect and gracious . . . or else they'd never let anyone else on. It was a question that I wasn't sure about then, and I'm still not sure to be honest. As culture shifts, so do expectations. The lines for acceptable behavior have never been static, and I was stumbling along in the dark without precedent.

Like all things, it just took time. While I wasn't always my best during the first two seasons of the show, things started getting better on season 3. With more experience, I started finding my feet.

I learned how to regulate my energy (without jelly beans) throughout a long shoot day. I finally asked for help with the rest of my life—scheduling, bills, taxes, cleaning, etc. Once M— and I stopped talking, I was no longer required to run everything by him and slowly started trusting my business-people with my professional affairs—which made everything smoother and was how it should have been in the first place. And then the studio implemented new, safer restrictions on overtime. So I was a little more rested too. By the final few seasons, M— was never on set and I was able to relax more. And once we hit syndication, I felt more secure about my finances and career.

After the fifth season, the numbers pointed to cancellation. We had poor ratings, and the last episode of the season had been written to function as a series finale. It was even confirmed that our original showrunner, Nahnatchka, was leaving the show after the fifth season. She already had her next job lined up. My management asked the network if we could pursue other acting projects for the fall too, in anticipation of the show's cancellation. While they didn't make any promises, they gave us their blessing to do so. Cancellation became a foregone conclusion. Though I'd grown to enjoy shooting *FOTB* in the later seasons, it felt like time. I was looking forward to a fresh start in a place that didn't hold so many memories of harassment and intimidation.

Right after *FOTB*'s assumed final season, the hit movie *Crazy Rich Asians* was released. Like *FOTB*, it was a groundbreaking moment for Asian American representation in Hollywood and a huge box office smash. And I'd starred in both, an accomplishment I was proud of. *CRA*'s success reignited the conversation on Asian American representation I'd become so familiar with during the first season of *FOTB*. People started to wonder: Would the network really cancel *FOTB* when *CRA* had been such a success? When everyone was talking about the dearth of Asian American representation in Hollywood? But numbers being numbers, I still thought the show would be canceled.

The news took us all by surprise. After finding out about the show's renewal on Twitter, I called my manager and he too was shocked. Because of my studio contract, I'd have to drop everything else—all the exciting jobs that the network had given us permission to pursue—and return to *FOTB*. The fresh start I'd looked forward to would have to wait. I hung up the phone. Suddenly, everything I'd held back for so long flooded the atmosphere and I became the microwaved tomato all over again. My feelings were overwhelming, a tsunami crashing through my body—betrayal, helplessness, like they'd lied to me. I had kept my head down and tolerated the discomfort for so long, trying to preserve everything for everybody else, and I just couldn't do it anymore. I needed to put my feelings somewhere other than my own body, which was at capacity. I didn't think about the lack of context, didn't care how bad it looked. From that first "no one wanted you" to every time M— said "you do what I say" to the crotch graze and which of my friends he'd fuck to the arm-fat jiggling to my withdrawal and isolation on set when I saw everyone being buddy-buddy with M— even after I'd told them he'd sexually harassed me, which meant they obviously didn't believe me. I didn't care how I sounded; I just needed to finally make a *sound*. I wasn't home in LA at the time, because I had just finished filming *Hustlers* in New York. So alone in my temporary rental apartment with no one to talk to, I unleashed all my built-up feelings on social media. The tomato finally burst.

The backlash was immediate. *Ungrateful bitch. How dare she. Boo-hoo poor actress has to go back to her high-paying job!* Then there was the schadenfreude that always follows a big social media scene. Seeing someone who was always so practiced suddenly lose control—was *entertainment*. I became a headline, a meme, a springboard for righteous opinion. An ungrateful girl making a scene.

I stopped looking at all social media, but I couldn't escape it. It was trending for weeks. Click counts made it newsworthy, and the story even began appearing on major news sites. It was on the TV at the gym. The sidewalk newsstands. Tabloids capitalized on the onslaught of internet hatred—vilifying me with groundless, salacious lies. A woman's perceived ingratitude became headline news.

Though I stopped looking at my social media accounts, I still received DMs through email. I apologized to a very upset former colleague of mine over DM. She replied with DM after DM shaming me . . . Telling me that nothing I could ever do would make up for my atrocious behavior and disgusting ingratitude. How I had sullied the one shining beacon of hope for Asian Americans. How selfish I was to not consider everyone else's jobs on the show. She demanded I bake cookies for and grovel at the feet of Randall and every single crew member of *FOTB* but said even that wouldn't be enough to make up for what I'd done. She told me how the show had been her nephew's favorite, and how I had ruined it for him. That I'd devastated him and I would never, ever be able to make up for it.

Her DMs made me feel helpless and desperate, my heart full of sharp tacks. Why wouldn't she believe my remorse? That I hurt as badly as she wanted me to? My head spinning, I realized I needed a wound to prove it, to prove that I hurt as bad as everyone said I deserved to hurt and it couldn't be a little wound, it had to be the biggest wound in the world for it to be enough. That's how I ended up clutching the balcony railing of my fifth-floor apartment and staring wildly down at the NYC street below with a reckless despair so total that my body ceased being a body and became a sound so dangerously high-pitched it was like nails on a chalkboard or a violin string pulled tight enough to cut flesh. The sound coursed through me and out of my fingertips like electricity as I started pulling myself over the railing, until a friend who'd come to check on me pried me from the balcony edge and dragged me to the elevator and down into a cab, where she breathlessly called my publicist for help because she was scared for my life, but also scared of doing the wrong thing. We were directed to the psychiatric ER of a mental hospital, where they took everything away from me and put me in a hospital gown. It was late at night. I was dizzy, my puffy eyes blurred by tear-engorged contact lenses, my mouth pasty with unbrushed teeth, my hair in shambles because they even took away my hair elastics for fear I'd hurt myself with them.

I spent that night on a cot in the empty waiting room, under surveillance. Weeping until the exhaustion wore me out.

The next morning, I told the two intake counselors what happened. That I almost jumped. That I'm very impulsive. (The edge of a balcony is not a place for impulsivity.) That I needed help.

Fresh Off the Boat changed my life, but not in the way you might expect. Sure, it got me out of debt and launched my career, but what really changed my life for the better was the hard stuff. The social media backlash and hospital stay made me finally get help. I found a therapist who'd worked with high-profile actresses and musicians and understood my unusual circumstances. Getting a new therapist wasn't as difficult as I'd thought; the retelling of stories wasn't tiring but, well . . . therapeutic. And it was through a daily, then tri-weekly session commitment to therapy that I clarified my values, learned how to allow my emotions without overwhelm, and developed better tools for managing big feelings. I still go to therapy once a week. I'm still learning, too.

A few months after those tweets, I went back to film what would become the final season of *FOTB*. I was nervous about returning. Not because of the public response, but because of the personal one—the cast and crew I'd worked with for more than a hundred episodes. I knew that first and foremost, I needed to make it right with the kids—the three boys who played my children on the show. *Fresh Off the Boat* was their world and pride. I knew what my actions had done to me, but what had it done to them?

So, during a photo shoot before we started filming, I pulled them aside. I'd carefully mapped out my words and remorse with my therapist, I wanted to be as good a mom as possible for them.

"I know there has been a lot of talk about some things I tweeted this summer," I began. "I'm sure you have had to deal with questions, and I am very sorry for that. I made a mistake. It wasn't a reflection of how I feel about you or about the show. I care so much about you. And I'm sorry you've had to deal with the repercussions of my words, you didn't deserve that, and it is my fault, I'm sorry." I kept repeating how sorry I was, felt like I couldn't say it enough.

I didn't want to cry, but I've never been able to stop my tears. They're always pulled out of me by an uncontrollable force, like magnets or the tide by the moon.

Forrest and Ian seemed a little uncomfortable—probably a normal reaction for teenage boys when adults break down in front of them. But Hudson, who played my oldest son, his face softening with so much love and forgiveness, said, "Hey . . . it's okay, Constance. We know you didn't mean it. We love you. It's okay. You're okay." He hugged me. My shoulders shook as I wept. He held me tighter. I'd played his mom for so long. When I first met him, he was four feet tall and full of feelings. But now he was over six feet tall, comforting his disgraced TV momma in his arms. "It's okay," he kept reassuring me, my gratitude for his forgiveness overwhelming me. Then, like a good big brother, he made Ian and Forrest come over and hug me too. I had come into that conversation with the intention of caring for my kids. And instead, my kid took care of *me*. I'll never forget that.

Next, I apologized to the rest of the cast, crew, producers, writers, and executives at the first table read of the season. Beforehand, I asked Justin, one of our producers, if it was okay for me to read an apology before we started. He said of course. After everyone had settled into the room, he stood up and said, "Constance has something to say and we need to listen to her." He hugged me and sat down, giving me the floor. It was so quiet. My hands shaking, I unfolded a piece of paper. I hadn't even started talking and I was already crying. Somehow, I finished reading the whole apology I'd written. It was the bravest thing I'd done in a long time. Maybe you will think that calling myself brave is tooting my own horn; go ahead and think that, I don't fucking care. The apology wasn't for you. It was for the people in that room. Chelsey held my hand as I read it. In a way, it felt like everyone in that room held my hand that day.

I'm lucky for those three kids, for the writing staff, for the wonderful crew, for Justin and Missy, the producers who always treated me well, but what I'm most lucky for is Randall. Having him as my costar for those tumultuous six years was like winning the lottery. I don't have enough words to ever express my enormous gratitude for his grace and patience. I am embarrassed I wasn't as wonderful as him, but I aspire to be, and know I'm getting better every day. In terms of how to be a good human being, he is my gold standard.

I never really spoke to M— again, but I eventually forgave him. And myself. We were both in high-pressure situations without precedents—it's only natural to stumble along the way. Hollywood has a history of mocking and belittling Asian men. It's hard to have big dreams in a culture that makes you feel small. And M— was always grasping at the things that made him feel big—his power as my boss, his constant name-dropping, his pleasure at "making offers." A lot was riding on the show, not just for Asian American representation, but for him personally. He'd been an assistant to a successful director for years, and *FOTB* was his first big show as a producer. I imagine he must have been under a lot of pressure, but he never talked about it. He was always trying so hard to be cool—maybe he felt like a good producer *had* to be. As someone who has tried and failed to be the cool girl for years, I don't envy that pressure. I'm not making excuses for him—just trying to understand him. Because when I do that, I stop blaming myself and feel better.

I've heard people claim that I've lost jobs over my tweets. Because when you're a public figure, perception impacts employment opportunities. But I'll never really know because I became pregnant during the final filming weeks of *FOTB*. I had a *rough* first trimester, often puking six times a day . . . so I couldn't take on any new projects. Then, a global pandemic happened. Then, I started to show. And once I gave birth to my daughter, I like, didn't really *want* to take on any new projects if they compromised quality time with my daughter. And those theoretical career opportunities I might have missed? Due to *tweets and tabloids?* Well. That means the jobs I've gotten since are from people who hire me for my ability and professionalism, rather than those who are swayed by false rumors or social media numbers. So in a way, the entire experience might have been a helpful filtering mechanism rather than a setback. I'd spent so much of my public life worried about what people thought of me. . . . It was freeing to finally let that go.

Today, I work on a TV show where I was able to begin with dignity and the confidence of experience. A true fresh start. I was welcomed on *The Terminal List* without intimidation or fear, and as a result, I feel like I get to be myself on a set. The producers and crew were supportive of my family needs from the get-go, carving out time for me to pump or breastfeed or hop on a call with the pediatrician. It films in Los Angeles, so I didn't have to uproot my family. My role on the show doesn't require as much press or media scrutiny and I am glad to just be able to focus on the acting part of it. I enjoy my work on the show and I feel good there.

———

Before *The Terminal List*, around the time I discovered I was pregnant, I began retreating from the public eye. I quit all social media and turned down magazine cover offers. I chose acting roles that wouldn't put me in the limelight too much—choices that have restored peace to my life. No longer hustling to be someone, posting to prove something, striving to get somewhere. I chuckle when I think of how my dreams used to be so big. Little did I know how much *better* the small things would be: The plain beauty of the breakfast table—my daughter's two-toothed grin, food on her face and all over the floor. Every new thing, a discovery. Watching her grow has been the greatest pleasure I've known.

M— has a daughter too, and back in our buddy days I remember a time when he joked: "I hope my daughter is a lesbian, so I don't have to deal with douchebags trying to get her when she grows up."

I didn't say my usual "ugh, you're such a dude." I didn't laugh either. In one of the few times I got to be myself, I just said, "Well, they say that girls usually date guys who are like their father. So, you know, just *be* the kind of person you'd want your daughter to date, and I think it will all turn out okay in the end."

I hope he's doing what I said.

At home in Virginia, 1990s

The Utmost Sincerity

It's easy to romanticize stuff you don't know jack shit about. And when I was a teenager living in the comfortable suburbs of Richmond, Virginia, that meant I romanticized hardship. I read writers like Plath, Kerouac, Hemingway. Listened to Ani DiFranco and Tori Amos. I even bought the piano sheet music for "Little Earthquakes" and played it on moody Sunday afternoons. It felt like my childhood had been one big air-conditioned grocery-store aisle—glossy magazines and twenty different brands of chewing gum. I longed to separate myself and become a deep, artistic individual.

So, around my senior year of high school, I started doing stereotypical artsy things. Wore all black, chain-smoked Gauloises, scowled at blondes. It wasn't unusual to hear me proclaim things like "Fuck society!" or "I only hang with people who read poetry!" I cut my hair lopsided with a pair of Fiskars scissors one Thursday night, crying out, "Vanity is bullshit!" to no one in particular. It was all bullshit, I thought. I pontificated that life, *real* life, could only be found away from the crowd—in the wilderness, in the sweat of labor, in the unknown and unexplored.

In my hometown, being a provocateur felt exciting and freeing. But once I left Virginia to study at an acting conservatory, it was less special. Soon, even arts college became comfortable and bland—the cable television and vegan grilled cheeses and snooty music tastes. Just like I'd felt the urge to separate myself from the ease of my suburban youth, now I longed to distinguish myself from the art school crowd. Like Thoreau, I dreamed of going to the woods to "live deliberately."

But I didn't know what I was trying to do, or how to do it. I wholeheartedly googled "how to build a log cabin by yourself," then wholeheartedly abandoned it as soon as the search results sprang up. Even though I wasn't Jewish, I considered going on a kibbutz, but the pictures made that look too hot and dusty. Unsure or scared or both, I was left pining after things that I had no clue about, and whining about comfort and privilege. Which, at the time, seemed almost as good as casting it off.

And that's how I ended up on a mountaintop on the other side of the world, living in a Buddhist monastery.

———

It was called the Humanstic Buddhist Monastic Life Program. My best friend Marrianne was the one who told me about it. She was a religion major at UVA, where they'd advertised the applications for it in her department. It was an immersive summer program for college students to experience life as Buddhist monastics. It was the program's inaugural year and it would take place at Fo Guang Shan, a monastery outside of Kaohsiung, Taiwan. *Perfect!* I thought, imagining this was my Walden Pond—the thing to separate me from the crowd again. None of the art school kids had lived at a Buddhist monastery. Religion had always fascinated me—the pure abandon that real faith required, the belief in things intangible and unprovable, how it made some people really good, but also made some people really bad. And while it was fashionable in my artsy-liberal crowd to moan about the hypocrisy and corruption of religion, Buddhism seemed like one of the few religions that was exempt from liberal critique.

Back then, the program was all-expenses-paid; they even covered airfare. This was very attractive to my broke ass, and I felt like that made it more legit than the profit-driven yoga retreats and meditation classes I'd seen advertised in New York. This program was conceived by a Buddhist nun named Yifa, a jolly, four-foot-ten Taiwanese woman with a wide-open smile and a PhD from Yale who once told me, laughing, "I don't like to pet animals. Even rabbits! Haha!" Ven. Yifa organized the program through Harvard Divinity School, where she was a visiting scholar.

Marrianne and I both applied: college transcript, personal essay, recommendations, etc. I knew I was at a disadvantage, not being academically inclined, but somehow, I got in. (Marrianne didn't, and it took a while for her to forgive me.) They accepted around thirty students that first year, most of whom were white Ivy League Americans majoring in religion. But there were a couple Canadians, a girl from Paris, someone from Brazil, I think. I was the only art school student. Most of us weren't Buddhist—you didn't have to be to enter the program. The purpose was education, not conversion.

Life at the monastery didn't require much. I packed one small suitcase with the basics: underwear, sunscreen, mosquito repellent, toothbrush. A point-and-shoot camera that used *film* (it was 2002). I didn't own a laptop at the time and smartphones hadn't been invented yet (the only people my age who had cell phones were rich kids with StarTACs). Then I got on a plane and flew to the other side of the world.

I was greeted at Kaohsiung International Airport by two monastics in caramel-colored robes. After some initial hellos and introductions, we climbed into a passenger van and a nun got behind the wheel. I don't know why I was surprised and delighted to see a Buddhist nun driving a van, but I was. Loved watching her drive, so petite she barely saw over the wheel. Loved how she got out of the van in her monastic robes to pump gas. As we drove away from the airport, the view outside the window went from city lights to tin shacks to country fields. Flat land and betel-nut stands every few miles. Betel-nut stands were small glass huts lit up in neon lights, each showcasing a betel-nut girl—girls in miniskirts and go-go boots who usually sat on stools, bored, reading magazines. (I'd later learn that betel nuts were a type of stimulant, like Red Bull/tobacco, that truck drivers chewed and spit to stay awake. The price of *one* betel nut cost ten times more than the price of five betel nuts. It was a code of sorts—you asked for five betel nuts if you wanted actual betel nuts. But if you asked for only *one* betel nut, the girl would "lean on your truck" and "chat" with you. Or at least that's what I was told. I thought it might be code for sex work, but I never asked.)

After miles and miles of country road, we began the drive up the mountain to the monastery that I would call home for the next several weeks.

I learned a lot of things that summer. Small acts of mindfulness—like how to fold my garbage into a tiny, tucked square to take up less space in a bin. How to gently lift and pull out a chair so it wouldn't create an obtrusive sound. How to bow: place palms together and kneel. Lower your forehead to the ground; keeping your forehead on the ground, extend your arms out in front of you, and rotate them to offer your palms up. Hold that position for a moment, then methodically stand back up in reverse order; finishing by touching your prayer hands to your forehead and then back down to your heart. How to sleep like a bow, stand like a tree, walk like the wind, sit like a bell.

Really! The monastics taught us to sleep curved *like a bow* on our right side so the heart was higher. To stand up straight and firmly rooted *like a tree*. Walking was *like the wind*—smooth, natural, and without artifice. And sitting, of course, was *in the shape of a bell*—cross-legged, hands in the center of your lap, palms on top of each other, thumbs linked to form an oval with your hands.

In a way, living at the monastery was how I imagine the military: order and rhythm to everything. We wore uniforms: plain twill button-up shirts with a sage-green trim, matching drawstring pants, navy-blue canvas sandals. We lived in small, spare dorms, four to a room. We followed a strict schedule, waking up early every morning to the sound of a mallet on a wooden board, a monastic walking up and down the halls in rhythm: *knock . . . knock . . . knock-knock*. After folding our bedding with instructed precision, we formed two silent lines in the hallway, boys on one side and girls on the other, in height order. Maintaining silence, we walked out to the courtyard for morning gongfu. It wasn't combative, but more of a morning stretch. A silent, monk-guided physical warm-up, as the white stone statues kept peaceful watch. We were always up before the sun so the mountain air was gray and opaque with humidity, so heavy you could feel it on your skin, like warm silk. After gongfu, we sat in the courtyard for our first of several meditation sessions each day. Cross-legged, eyes closed, mindful quiet in the warm morning fog.

The quiet was finally broken at breakfast. While our other meals were eaten in silence with the rest of the monastics in the refectory, our morning meal took place in a small classroom. It was a Western-style breakfast buffet where we were free to chat and eat like normal college students. Then we returned to our dorms to brush our teeth, shower, or go up to the roof, where we'd wash the previous day's uniforms in plastic tubs, hanging them up on clotheslines to dry in the sun.

Our days consisted of scheduled lectures, Buddhism classes, meditation, and various monastery activities. Sometimes we participated in community service—going down the mountain and into the city to help paint nursing homes, play with kids at a local day care, help with translation, or weed in the Zen garden.

Lunch was a unique experience. We ate with all the monks and nuns who lived at the monastery. It took place in the refectory—a building that looked like an old gymnasium from the seventies, with tall ceilings and industrial fans. The refectory was filled with long tables that were preset in this order (left to right): broth bowl, plate, rice bowl, piece of fruit. At noon sharp, you entered the refectory in neat, silent lines, pulling out your stool as quietly as possible. Everyone sat facing the front. After an initial chant, lunch was taken in complete silence, nothing but the faint clicking of ceramic plates and chopsticks. It was mindful, intentional eating, which somehow made the bland vegetarian food taste really good. When you were eating, *you were eating*. It's a ritual I sometimes miss, when I see people eating meals with scattered attention—scrolling on their phones or reading the news.

Dinner was also in the refectory, but it was a smaller affair because many of the monastics fasted at night. We were encouraged to do the same, which I sometimes did, sometimes didn't. After dinner, we had free time until evening vespers. There was a little cart down by the monastery mountain gate that sold souvenirs and ice cream. Sometimes, instead of dinner, I went there and bought a Chinese brand of white chocolate wrapped in clear cellophane. Buttery and soft from the heat, I'd finish the whole thing on the walk back up to the monastery, licking my fingers and carefully folding the wrapper in a tightly packed square before discarding it in a bin.

The monastery was expansive, and I liked strolling the different temples, shrines, and gardens during free time. Going to the main shrine was a tonic. Before entering, you removed your shoes and the stone floor felt nice and cool under your feet. Its cavernous ceiling and dim lighting were a soothing retreat from the white heat outside. The walls were lined, floor to ceiling, with dark Buddha statues in front of wall carvings, through which the air flowed in, and you could glimpse the sky. There was the faint smell of incense and the quiet padding of bare feet as monastics tended the shrine and laypeople explored and worshipped. Sometimes I'd bow over and over, eyes closed, enjoying the trancelike repetition and the cool stone floor on my forehead.

At the very top of the mountain was a little garden where it was blazing hot because the sun was direct on all sides and the plants grew close to the ground, offering no shade. I remember the first time a few of us made the long hike up there. I was listless from the heat, clothes drenched in sweat, my brow knit as I futilely fanned myself with my hand. I wanted to whine about the heat *soooo* much, but whining is not very Buddha-like, so I refrained. And the nun who tended the garden, who had been there all day, whose monastic robes were much heavier than my thin cotton uniform? She never whined, even as continual beads of sweat dropped from her jaw. Calm and practical, she was glad for our company, welcoming us to sit at a low wooden table where she offered us a cup of tea. A cup of *hot* tea.

"The heat of the tea inside your body will make the heat of the outside seem less severe," she said.

———

Though I felt restless on occasion, I liked the structure of monastery life. Enjoyed having an assigned community and scheduled activities. It was a relief to not feel like you were a loser if you didn't have plans on a Saturday night.

The program culminated in a weeklong meditation retreat. Complete silence and only meditation for an entire week. We'd even sleep in the meditation hall—in padded cubbies behind our meditation cushions. The retreat was optional, with most students dropping out after the first day or so. I went through the whole week and my experience varied on different days. The first day, I felt clear and vigorous, like how you feel after aerobic exercise. The second day I wanted to crawl out of my skin, bang my head against the wall, throw something across the room. It took everything in me not to physically freak the fuck out. Though I remained calm on the outside, my insides were lashing out. It felt like an itch you wanted to scratch but the itch is not on your body but in the air, in your blood, in the entire world and you can't fucking scratch it because it's everywhere and your hands are nothing. And you don't care why it itches, you just care that it gets scratched but it *can't*. Even now, just remembering the feeling puts my insides on edge. But somehow, I made it through that day. The internal violence of it clouded my mind, like a muddy puddle in perpetual agitation. But on the third day, the dirt settled, and the water began to clear.

Though most of our meditation was in silence, on the third day, a monk talked us through a guided meditation. For those of us who didn't understand Chinese, they offered foam headphones, where it would be translated, live, into English. Because I understand Chinese only at the level of a toddler, I used the headphones.

My favorite monk translated. I wish I could remember his name, but I can't, so I'm calling him Bud. Bud the Buddhist monk. He was a white guy from New Jersey who had come to Kaohsiung by way of South Africa. He was tall and thin and had a dry sense of humor that stopped juuuust short of smugness. He'd given a wonderful lecture earlier in the summer, beginning with "CNN is the drug of America" and ending with "it doesn't matter what religion you practice, so long as you practice it with the utmost sincerity. And if that doesn't work out for you, welp, then may I be reborn a cow!" And we'd all laughed. Listening to him translate was wonderful. His gentle voice, so intimate through those head-phones, felt as if he were whispering not words in your ear but breath on your heart, your scalp, the soles of your feet.

We were instructed to meditate on the idea of a dead body. It sounds morbid, but what is more natural than death? After some time and breath, I began to understand the body in a new way and the air around me stopped itching. It wasn't even air . . . but simply a continuation of me, the cushion, the floor, the soil of the mountain, the rocks below that, the dead body in decay, every body that ever was. "Interconnectedness" is the word some Buddhists use for it, but language falls short.

After that guided meditation, the rest of the days were just flow. My mind hummed with the insects outside. My breath rose and fell with ocean currents. For the first time in my life, it felt like every single cell of my body was oxygenated, hydrated, and nourished to its most perfectly optimal level.

There are no shortcuts for the true things in life. You have to *sit through* the discomfort. Sometimes, you have to sit through it for a very, very long time.

———

In general, I'm not all that Zen-like. I'm no more evolved or disciplined than the next guy; in fact, as a procrastinator and lazy person, I'm probably less disciplined than many. After that summer at the monastery, I'd eventually go back to being my normal self—worrying about tweezing upper lip hairs or boys texting me back—but for the rest of that meditation retreat week there was peace and flow. This has not happened for me in subsequent meditation sessions. Then again, I've never spent more than an hour in meditation since then, let alone a full week.

After I left the monastery, I went back to New York City, where I lived with my boyfriend. The experience was jarring. Traffic, billboards, subway cars, mirrors, sex, the radio, my family and peers and their questions and enthusiasm. Even the foliage of the city trees felt agitated. The air became itchy again. Only now there were so many distractions to scratch it. Night clubs, money, substances, jealousy. In New York, I didn't have to sit and suffer through the itch.

And then the itch wasn't an itch anymore; it was impatience, and then impatience wasn't impatience but ambition. Rushing wasn't rushing anymore; it was productivity. *What's so wrong with that?* I rationalized. *What is wrong with goals and productivity?* I stopped meditating because there were things I needed to do . . . waitressing to pay rent, exercising so I could have what I perceived to be the body of a castable actress and desirable human. I was hustling to get somewhere, be somebody. Everything became goal-oriented or character defining. Even the monastery and its lessons became an adornment—something I could talk about to make me seem interesting.

And for a while, that's how I used it—to impress people. It always worked. *Wow—you lived at a Buddhist monastery. . . . Was it life changing?!* And while I was proud of it at first, people's reactions began to fatigue me. In their impressed faces, I could see the way they romanticized the religion the way I'd once done too. I couldn't ever match their awe. Or I was jealous of it. Then I'd become irritated and attempt to do whatever was the opposite of romanticizing it. Then I'd become disgusted by my own irritation, knowing it was borne of arrogance, impatience, a bitter heart. Next, I'd become disgusted by my own ego and vanity for even bragging about the monastery in the first place. That those qualities were so reflexive in me left me feeling like maybe I was just a bad person. That bad-person feeling happened so gradually that there's no one moment to pinpoint its genesis. . . . But I do remember the moment when I realized exactly what I'd lost. I realized it through a cheese ball.

―――――――

Yes. An actual ball of cheese. You know those big, gummy orange cheese balls, usually rolled in crushed almonds and served on a plastic platter next to salami and Ritz Crackers? That kind of cheese ball.

I was home in Virginia for the holidays when my dad asked me to come to a Christmas party that a church member was throwing. I knew those parties were always full of bland, chipper conservative folks. But I was bored. So I put down my book of David Foster Wallace essays and begrudgingly went along. Maybe there'd be wine. It was in a small suburban home—old carpeting, Christmas tree, family portraits, two-liter sodas, and a platter with a cheese ball in the middle of it. I remember looking at that cheese ball with disgust. In my *real* life in New York City, where I worked at a *French* restaurant, we had cheese like Roquefort and Morbier. Not this preservative-laden ball of sodium shit.

"Isn't this tasty?" the party host, a friendly, middle-aged white man asked, attempting polite conversation. I looked at his cheap argyle sweater vest, cracker crumbs lightly dusting his belly, and nodded politely. I was already bored.

"Your dad tells me you're an actress! I always wondered how y'all memorize all those lines," he exclaimed, looking impressed.

A familiar irritation stirred in me. I gave him a tight smile. "All part of the job!"

Though he sensed my irritation, he remained kind. "Well, we're glad you're here. Thank you for coming," he said.

After he walked away, I rolled my eyes. I felt so above it.

Then he cleared his throat and gathered us all for prayer. On cue, everyone formed a circle and held hands. Quiet and warm smiles all around, they began to pray: "Dear Lord Jesus, thank you for these friends and this food. . . ."

The urge to roll my eyes again was overwhelming, but instead I watched them pray. Normal, suburban folks giving thanks for cheese balls and for each other. Suddenly, an un-expected wave of shame flooded through me—*why couldn't I just leave it the fuck alone?* I had culture, experience, travel, stylish boots on my feet, and interesting books in my bag, but I was mean and judgmental. I couldn't even let someone pray without scoffing at them. Then I remembered what Bud had said about how to worship. . . . And here it was, right in front of me in this carpeted living room in my hometown: *the utmost sincerity*.

I may have lived at a Buddhist monastery, but I wonder if the Christian cheese ball guy got it better than I ever did.

———

It's a question I continue to grapple with as internet vigilance and scrutiny takes the shine off things. The girl who romanticized hardship has been upgraded to a woman who thinks about socioeconomic privilege, systemic and structural racism—and the ways she has benefited from and even contributed to those systems. True self-awareness requires context, and I'm glad to know it. Today, I recognize how grossly privileged and naive it was for me to idealize hardship. But I have to admit it makes me a little wistful when I think about the dumb, angsty teenager I used to be. I remember how vital it all felt to her then. How her heart was soft and fresh and full of energy and confusion. She may have cut her hair ragged to decry vanity, but she was also the girl who pored over *Seventeen* magazine for makeup tips. She may have said she wanted to live in the woods like Thoreau, but then she could barely stand a hot day in the monastery garden.

Buddhism tells us that attachment causes suffering. Buddhists meditate and practice nonattachment to cease suffering. But I was an angsty, arty young person who romanticized suffering. . . . I *sought it out*. The exact opposite of what Buddhism teaches! If attachment is suffering and I romanticized suffering—was I *seeking out* attachment all along?

As a teenager, I thought I needed to get away from the crowd. But maybe what I truly wanted was something else entirely.

One winter after I'd been living in New York City for a few years, I started going to Quaker church services, or "Friends Meetings," as they are called. On Sunday mornings, I took the subway to Union Square and walked to the plain wooden parish on Fifteenth Street by Stuyvesant Square Park.

In Quakerism, you are considered a minister of your own faith. There is no leader—no priest, no pastor. No sermon, no lecture or music. It's a lot like meditation in that the entire service is spent in mostly silence. People speak only if they are moved to. Only a few people ever spoke. Sometimes, I wanted to, but whenever I thought I might, my heart would pound, and my face would flush with fear that I'd sound dumb; that they'd kick me out. I don't know why I thought that; everyone was always listened to with respect and care. There was an old man who, pushing himself up with the aid of his walker, grumbled loudly for a few minutes at the end of every meeting. Even though he seemed kinda grumpy and you could never understand anything he was saying, everybody listened. No judgment, just sincere attention. That's how it was in that room with the plain white walls and gentle sunlight flowing in through the mullioned windows. Time and grace. I remember how the tree branches outside those windows moved, flowers fluttering. How, toward the end of the Friends Meeting, the children returned from their Sunday school classes, quietly sliding into the pews next to their parents. How the parents' faces softened as their kids crawled into their laps, or snuggled in their arms.

I'd smile at the children, trying to emote the same parental warmth and happiness. But inside, I was often sad. I was always alone at these services. It felt too weird asking my artsy liberal friends to go to church; they all liked to claim that religion was corrupt bullshit.

After a few weeks, I stopped going to the Quaker church. Just like at the monastery and the cheese ball party, I was never able to feel like I really belonged there. The few times I was approached, post–Quaker meeting, by friendly folks introducing themselves, my heart pounded and my palms sweated. I smiled and stumbled away from them as fast as I could, half laughing and half mumbling excuses about needing to be somewhere. I don't know why I was so ashamed of my loneliness. Why I ran away from the one thing I wanted so much.

Playing Hermia in *A Midsummer Night's Dream*

Dressing Wounds

George and I first met in 2006. We were in the same Shakespearean acting workshop, where I was a student, and he was a teaching assistant. I didn't know it then, because I was dating Rob (aka Buck), but George would become one of the great loves of my life. He was tall and smart and really cool. His face had a soft, attentive stillness. He made me laugh a lot, and we liked the same books for the same reasons. One night, another actor pointed at George and whispered to me, "You guys are supposed to be together." I shook my head. "You're crazy. I'm in love with my boyfriend." And I was! After that acting workshop, George and I went our separate ways. Nothing ever having happened. We became Facebook friends but didn't even message each other for a couple years.

A few years later, newly single, I met George for dinner at a restaurant in the West Village called Employees Only. Talking with him was pleasurable and easy. It turned into an eight-hour date during which we kept getting kicked out of places. Out of the restaurant, because we stayed too long, and they needed the table. The next bar, because they were closing. The bar after that, because we were kissing too much. It was the most fun date ever and I fell for him, hard.

He went to West Virginia to teach a summer workshop. The first couple weeks he was there we talked for hours on the phone every night until we decided to split the cost of a short flight for me to meet him there. It was nice living with him outside the city for a bit. We read books next to each other, drank cheap Old Grand-Dad whiskey, made sandwiches out of soft bread and cold cuts, watched the Olympics on TV. One weekend, we drove to Fallingwater and looked at a beautiful thing that humans built. It opened up something in us, and during the drive home, we talked. About our families, our feelings, our pasts. We wondered about our futures. I told him about how Mrs. Kantor accused me of plagiarism in middle school and how it broke me. He told me how he loved playing chess as a child, but his elementary school principal chided him, saying, "Ha! You may know the rules of chess. But you don't *really* know how to play." He'd felt so embarrassed that he never played again. Stories about acting school, first feelings of shame, what it felt like to have been deemed a "gifted" child. In that cheap rental car, we learned each other. I still remember the white-gray sky and his dark hair. His face gazing ahead as he drove. It was a wonderful trip, and I went back to New York totally in love.

My love made me hot with demands and desire. It had the opposite effect on George. He became cold. A coolness he validated with coarse logic, shrugs, and judgment. Suddenly, the guy who would hold my face in the morning and say,

"I'm so happy you're here," wasn't even texting me. Would take six hours to respond. No longer cared to initiate plans. He didn't do anything *blatantly* incriminating, but after such a real connection, his casual withholding felt bewildering and punitive. It was ghosting before ghosting was a thing.

And then it was over. It was quick; he did it over the phone. I remember sitting on the floor of my third-floor walk-up on Eighty-Fifth Street. My bedroom windows faced a dark air shaft, and the air was the type of gray that felt black. I hung up the phone and stared at the lavender wall. I felt like that Jack Gilbert poem where he says "my heart is as helpless as crushed birds."

In my experience, there are two options for dealing with a wounded heart. The first is numbing and avoidance: alcohol, drugs, casual sex. This can be a temporary reprieve, but if you're not careful, that recklessness can harden you. Make you feel brave in false ways. The second option—the one I've found to be most helpful—is to accept the heartbreak and use it to instruct you. It's the more painful option, but its effects are beautifully effusive. So often, we equate our identities with Things: a job, a boyfriend, a fashion choice, our untouchable taste in music. But when we're stripped of Things, it forces us to reckon with our true identities. Who are we without those Things? Since I was a teenager, I always had a boyfriend. But suddenly, left without George in my life, I felt aimless and insignificant.

After that breakup, I immediately booked a one-way ticket to Los Angeles. As a die-hard New Yorker, I hated LA on principle; had sworn I'd never live there. But I told myself I was going to try a different approach to my acting career. In truth, it was my way of avoidance: you don't have time to lick your wounds when you're dealing with the logistics of a cross-country move. I needed to get as far away as I could, to a place where I had no history. LA was a place where I had nothing. Without any money to move or buy an airplane ticket, I put it on my almost-maxed-out credit card, paying the minimum for years.

The first year I lived in LA, I sort of sleepwalked around in the sunny smog, constantly wondering what George was doing. Thinking of his life more than my own. In hindsight, that's pathetic as fuck, but it's also an honest account of my mental space. The only thing worse than doing a pathetic thing is pretending as though that's not what you're doing. I'd avoided, numbed, tried to outrun the pain . . . it was time to finally accept it and try to learn something from it.

The love George and I'd shared made me feel real and seen. When I finally accepted that he didn't love me back anymore my shoulders dropped and my breathing softened. *That's okay*, I told myself, *I'm sad, but I'm okay. I'm still me—I can still love.* And that's when I decided to love George without reciprocation. Without contact or communication. Instead, I learned to see his face in every face I met. To regard those faces with compassion for the journeys that we're all trudging through. That empathy bled into my work in a wonderful way. I started meeting my acting auditions with that same tender care, as opposed to my previous patterns of anxiety and approval-seeking. It made my work flourish in a way that was alive and open. It worked better than avoidance, and finally, finally, I got over him.

A year later, he wrote me an email, apologizing for his behavior. Promising an explanation later. He never did explain, but he didn't need to. I'd already forgiven him. Over the next seven years, from across the country, George and I built a friendship. We had hours-long phone calls late into the night. I've always loved sending handwritten letters, and I especially loved writing them to him. I met and fell deeply in love with a man in Los Angeles and was with him for four years. George met someone too. It didn't drift us apart; we were happy for each other. It made us even better friends, because there was more freedom and trust when the possibility of romantic love wasn't there.

When I suddenly went from poor waitress to successful actress, everyone around me had their own ideas about how I was supposed to feel. Even my well-intentioned then boyfriend was honestly baffled at my paranoia, loneliness, and fear. He didn't understand why I wasn't excited by all the attention. Only George allowed me the space to have complex and uncomfortable feelings about fame. He never tried to "save" me during my crises. Never tried to fix things. Instead, he held a deep faith in my navigation of my newfound visibility while simultaneously hearing my complicated fears about it. That's not an easy thing to do. He did it beautifully. During that time, I'd often call him in a hyperventilating panic, and by the end of the conversation, I would be breathing easy, laughing.

Then, one day, a few months after I had gone through a breakup, George suggested I visit him in Ireland, where he was teaching. I hadn't seen him in more than seven years. It had only been phone calls, letters. I said yes and called my therapist. She blessed the reunion.

I flew to London, had a three-hour layover where I did a sheet mask to moisturize my skin, flew to Dublin as it became dark, took a bus from the airport to Dublin center, texted him my location, sat down with a book, and waited about five minutes until he walked up to me. He looked at me with disbelief and love. "You're really here," he said, his face opening up. We went to a little pub around the corner from his place. After some initial nerves, we kissed and it was like old times again. The love had been there all along. It felt like being young without the stupid parts of being young.

After that week in Dublin, we still lived in separate cities, but I flew to see him in New York whenever I had a week off. Being intimate again after ten years of connection, I asked us to commit to each other. For him to be my boyfriend. I wasn't asking for the moon. People had committed for less, and over longer distances. But just like before, he disdained the restricting language of commitment. And hey, I know it's

uncool to care so much about language. But I've always been
uncool. And I really, *really* cared about this language. We got
in a fight about it. He talked me out of it, using the distance
as an excuse, so I backed off. I tried to rationalize his logic,
but it didn't work for me. I tried again and he told me he
wanted to be able to sleep with other people.

"But I love you and still want to be with you too," he said.
I got upset. I just wanted him to be my boyfriend.
He said he'd think about it.

THE SCENE: *WAITING FOR A COMMITMENT*

*CONSTANCE, mid-thirties, sits on an empty stage. The
stagelights illuminate only her head and shoulders, so the
rest of the stage remains cloaked in darkness.
She addresses the audience:*

CONSTANCE
Then, he became cold again, not
communicating with me for five days.
Again, nothing *blatantly* incriminating, but
in context, those five days of silence had a
bewildering, punitive feeling that was all too
familiar. I tried really hard to be the cool girl
who doesn't call first, but I've never been
cool.

And I broke.

(The lights go out. Things shift in the darkness, we hear a phone number being dialed. As it rings, a spotlight comes up on the face of Constance, stage left. We still see just her head and shoulders, a phone held up to her ear. It rings for a long time. When someone finally answers, a spotlight comes up on the face of George, stage right, phone to his ear.)

GEORGE

Hey.

CONSTANCE

Hi!

GEORGE

Hi!

(A long beat.)

CONSTANCE

So? Like, have you thought about it?
Because I'm worth the commitment, George.
We've loved each other for so long. It's not
like we don't know each other. Or like we
haven't been through this before. And I just,
it's been so hard these past few days. I haven't
heard anything from you. And this isn't fair,
George. Please don't do this to me again.
Can we just give it a shot, please? I know

the distance is hard but can we just try? I
love you. I want to be with only you. And
if it doesn't work, then it doesn't work . . .
but we'll only know if we *try*. We owe it to
ourselves to try. You'll never regret trying. Can
we please try? Please? We love each other!

GEORGE

First off, calm down. You haven't even asked
me how my past few days have been. It's not
always about you.

CONSTANCE

Oh. Sorry. You're right. What's been going
on?

GEORGE

Well *(chuckles)*. Ho boy. I mean . . . *rough* on
my end.

CONSTANCE

(hopeful)

Yeah? You too?

GEORGE

The dean called me in.

CONSTANCE

(thrown)

    Oh. Why, what happened?

GEORGE

    Well, apparently, it came to his attention that
    one of my female students has a crush on
    me. She told another student that she would
    do anything to sleep with me and a teacher
    overheard it and that teacher reported it to
    the dean. So the dean called me in to talk to
    me about it.

CONSTANCE

    . . . Oh gosh.

GEORGE

    I know, how *awful*, right? I mean, I obviously
    didn't do anything, but it completely
    delegitimizes me and my teaching. But I don't
    really know what else to do. I want to inspire
    my students, but I can't control it if they
    misinterpret it, you know?

*(The spotlight dims on George as he babbles on and on.
Constance addresses the audience.)*

CONSTANCE

(aside)

Looking back, I'm amazed at my patience
with his unconscious humblebragging
about his sexual value. I mean, of course I
wanted him to share his life and problems
with me. But the timing of this was, at best,
insensitive and, at worst, suspect. But I didn't
say anything, because I honestly didn't feel
threatened by this student, just vaguely
annoyed at his lack of self-awareness. But,
hey, we all get caught up in our own little ego
games sometimes, so instead I just said

(Spotlight comes back up on George, as she addresses him.)
I'm sorry. That must be hard.

GEORGE

Yeah. Though I should have realized. Before
all this, I actually bumped into her at a
holiday party, dunno why she was there. But
we had a nice, long conversation. Maybe she
mistook that as flirting.

CONSTANCE

Oh, huh. Maybe you could have told her
about me?

GEORGE

Constance.

CONSTANCE

What?! We're dating. We're in love. We've
been in love for fifteen years.

GEORGE

That's personal—it's nobody else's business.
I don't need to be constantly talking about
who I'm dating all the time.

CONSTANCE

You mean like *I* do.

GEORGE

. . .

*(Lights dim on George as Constance addresses the audience
again.)*

CONSTANCE

(aside)

And I did. I talked about him all the time
because I loved him so much and I am not
embarrassed of my heart and its boldness.
Well, actually, I am embarrassed all the time,
but I do it anyway. Why didn't he mention

me to that student? I know it's uncool to constantly talk about your boyfriend or girlfriend, but did he need to be cool *that badly*? It would have been a kind, innocuous hint to the woman.

This is why the language of commitment was important. Bingo!

(back to George)

This is why the language of commitment is important, George. I want us to commit to each other with *language*. Me asking for that is not ridiculous or shameful or immature, even though somehow you make me feel like it is?

GEORGE

I never said that.

CONSTANCE

No, I guess you didn't. Sorry. George, we've loved each other for so long. Why can't we just try for once? All I want is to be boyfriend-girlfriend. Why is that so bad?

GEORGE

I just . . . I don't want to set myself up for future pain.

CONSTANCE

Can we talk about this more when you're in
LA next week?

GEORGE

Oh, I meant to tell you, I'm not coming to LA
anymore.

CONSTANCE

. . .

GEORGE

I just don't think it's a good idea.

*(Lights dim on George as Constance addresses the
audience.)*

CONSTANCE

(aside)

I didn't think my heart could break any
further, but there it was. He wouldn't even
make time to fly from New York to LA? After
all the times I had flown to see him? I'd gone
to West Virginia, Dublin, New York, and I
would have kept going.

(back to George—heartbroken)

So, what does this mean for us? What do we
do?

GEORGE

(encouraging, casual)

> Keep texting, keep talking, keep sending fun
> gifs. I dunno.

(click. As George hangs up the phone, his side of the stage goes dark.)

CONSTANCE

(to audience)

> Those were his last spoken words to me.
> As a final attempt I sent him a long email
> pleading to meet me halfway. He ignored it.
> A day later, he just sent me a kissing heart
> emoji. That's it. Logic and coolness were
> his fortresses and the walls were up. The
> more things change, the more they stay
> the same.

> And that's how I ended up here.

(The lights come up on the rest of the stage, and we see she's sitting on her bed, discarded papers strewn all about her. She's writing a letter. She checks her phone—nothing. She continues writing. She looks out into the audience.)

CONSTANCE

> It's been three days since his last text. Not
> a lot, I guess. But when you're used to

spending hours on the phone every night with
someone, three days of silence feels like an
awful lot. So I guess you could say, I had a lot
on my mind.

*(She checks her phone again. Stares at her notepad. Licks
her thumb to count the pages.)*

CONSTANCE

One, two, three, four-five-six, seven, eight,
nine . . . ten! Ten pages' worth! Jesus.

*(She holds up the ten-page letter in the air, shaking her
head. Checks her phone again.*
A beat, as she rereads the letter. Rips it in two. Laughs.)

CONSTANCE

More, actually. This is, like, my sixth draft.
And it's been condensed from the original.

*(She gestures grandly toward the scattered papers on the
floor.)*

CONSTANCE

Sixty-plus handwritten pages of pathetic.

(She picks up one letter and gestures toward it.)
In this one I'm just talking about how much I
love him.

(picks up another)

In this one I'm apologizing for overreacting
and pressuring him.

(picks up another, reads it)

Ha, in this one I'm showing off—trying to get
deep and philosophical so he'll realize how
great I am.

(picks up another)

I'm saying goodbye in this one. Huh.

(picks up another two)

This one is basic manipulation; this one is
begging.

And these . . .

*(She walks over to a box on a bookshelf, pulls out three
thin letters; one is actually a postcard.)*

are all the letters he's written to me over the
past fifteen years. Three.

*(A beat, as she looks at the meager three letters next to her
piles of drafts.)*

That's when I realized, this fucker doesn't
deserve all these pages. And he doesn't
deserve the girl that wrote them. Why was
I doing this to myself again? Hadn't pain
instructed me years ago? Shouldn't *he* finally

receive some instruction? He's getting a
fucking email.

(She moves to her laptop and begins typing.)

I did it coldly over email one afternoon:

> To: George
> Subject: (none)
>
> Hey . . . this isn't working. Let's stop picking this back up.
> The vagueness is just not healthy or kind. So, for clarity: I
> no longer want to be friends with you, I'm going to move
> on with my life. No need to respond. I wish you all the
> best.
>
> Take care,
> Constance

I clicked send. Numb, I drove to meet friends for lunch.
Sat down in a bright café, blinked at the menu. Calmly told
my friends that I had just broken up with my favorite person
in the world and then promptly wept over a plate of vegan
nachos. I ended it all, the relationship, the friendship, the
fifteen-year bond. It hurt so much.

———

On a phone call during our friendship years, I once asked
George if I helped him at all, added to his life in any way.
This was back when I had all those complicated feelings

about fame and he was the only one who understood. I told him how he brought so much to my life, but I wasn't sure I did that for him. Did I? He became quiet, almost tender. "Yes," he said. Nothing more. Just *yes*.

I never did find out how.

I think that somewhere, even way back when I was dating Buck, I had always hoped that George was the one. It took me years to let that hope die. I know it's pathetic. I know that a commitment-phobe dude is nothing original, and even less original is the love I will always carry for him. It's lame and uncool. And trust me, I *wish* that I was writing something empowered and flossy and fierce here. But who am I kidding, all I can be is me. And I'm uncool.

The breakup was clean, the way I had asked for it to be (he was always respectful of my requests). I didn't call or drunk text or like his posts or anything. I unfollowed him on all social media, and then I disappeared from social media entirely. It's been years since I've seen him or heard his voice. On Election Day of 2020, he texted me: Thinking of you today, hope you are healthy and happy.

I didn't want to ignore it, but I knew it shouldn't continue either, so I texted back: Thanks! I'm doing really good. Hope you are too.

He "loved" the text, and that's the last of our communication.

I'm grateful for all of it. I loved hard. Hurt hard, too. I learned a lot. Even our second breakup, pathetic as it was, kind of makes me proud. I'm proud that, despite everything,

I opened my heart enough to get hurt again. I feel brave. It's been so long, but I sometimes wonder if he suffered over it or if his pain-protection plan worked.

After our first breakup, right before I moved to LA, George and I went out for a farewell drink. He'd broken up with me a few months prior and had no idea that I'd booked a one-way ticket to LA. We sat down at the bar, and I was able to act cool for about two minutes before I was overcome with emotion.

"I am leaving New York because you broke my heart!" I cried. I was sloppy and embarrassing, crying at the zinc bar. He listened to me with his still, attentive face. He held my hand, his eyes full of care. I snatched it away, crying like a child. I told him how it wasn't fair that he had made such an impact on me, but I'd hardly touched him at all.

"You did, though," he said, holding my hand again. "I just go through it differently."

I said I didn't believe him! How could he be so calm! I got upset. I told him I wanted to punch him in the face, give him a black eye—if I couldn't impact him emotionally, I wanted to do it physically.

He said, "You should. I deserve it."

Later, we got drunk and had sex, and after, I said I still wanted to punch him. I'd never punched anyone before.

"You should do it," he said.

"I really want to," I said.

"Do it, punch me," he said.

"I am going to," I said.

His face twisted into a mixture of apology and self-loathing and callous disregard. "DO IT," he said. So, I pulled back my fist and socked him in the face, breaking his skin. He started bleeding from his brow bone.

"You told me to do it!" I cried, immediately filled with guilt.

He became calm—like somehow the punch had given him some peace. "Yes, I did," he said. "It's okay." He didn't get angry or upset. He sighed and held me closer and fell asleep, his arms still around me.

I gently nudged my way out of bed. I came back with cotton and Neosporin and Band-Aids. I cleaned and bandaged his wound as he slept. We would end up telling each other that story a lot during our long friendship. How I gave him a black eye, how he still has a scar. It was outrageous and funny and totally *us*. I always felt a twinge of shame about it. But I think that's why we laughed. It was nice to laugh. To be forgiven, to forgive. Whenever he retold the story he always marveled at one thing: "My favorite part," he'd say, his face softening, "was that you dressed my wound. You dressed my wound as I slept." Saying it as though I was the kindest person in the world.

In the children's choir of
Joseph and the Amazing Technicolor Dreamcoat

An Apology

There's boatloads of evidence so I might as well get ahead of it and tell you all now: I am guilty of sexual harassment. Of *being* the harasser. Yes. Me. I will tell you what I did. And you might think it's not a big deal. A harmless joke. But I shouldn't have done it and I tried to stop doing it, but it was hard. I had a problem: I couldn't stop writing the word "penis."

On *Fresh Off the Boat*, every time you saw my character writing on a legal pad, signing a check, or making a grocery list, I was writing the word "penis" over and over again. I wasn't discreet about it either; everyone knew. There's even video evidence, because at the end of a scene or a take, I'd always show the camera my penis-strewn paper and giggle. The proof was everywhere. "Penis" was written all over my character's props.

It started in season 1. There was a joke, written in the script, where one of the boys is eating alphabet cereal and the word "boob" floats out in cereal on his spoon.

It's a juvenile, harmless joke. But I was, like, *in a mood* that day, so in my head I was like, *Why is it okay for a woman's body part to be a joke, but not a man's?* Sometimes, I just get in a mood, y'all. I decided that day that if "boob" was okay to joke about, then "penis" should be too. At the time, it felt like a righteous statement. Children should not grow up thinking that ridiculing a woman's body was normal but that a man's vulnerable parts were off-limits. But still, I shouldn't have done it. Two wrongs don't make a right; two boobs don't make a peen.

And the thing is, I'm actually a fan! I *adore* penii. In this book, I've mentioned penises several times in different ways. This wasn't by design; it just happened. So, they're obviously on my mind. Like I said, I'm a fan.

I thought maybe I could get away with it because I used the anatomical word and not slang. I never, ever wrote "dick" or "cock" or "prick." Only "penis." "Boob" is slang and I *never* used slang. I never drew lewd pictures either. Just the word, the letters: P-E-N-I-S. Usually in cursive. I've only ever done this on *Fresh Off the Boat* and never on any other job I've had. I'm a serious actress.

Anyway, I did it for three and a half seasons of *Fresh Off the Boat* until someone complained to Justin, one of the producers, that it was inappropriate. Justin pulled me aside for a talk. He felt bad because he knew I thought it was harmless fun, but he had to tell me that it made someone uncomfortable. I think he expected me to protest, to defend myself and say, "It's a joke! Everybody laughs!" But I didn't defend myself. I just said, "I'm glad you told me, and you are right, I shouldn't have done that. I will stop. I'm sorry."

I may have been joking, and sure, everyone laughed, but laughter is not an excuse. Sometimes people laugh when they're uncomfortable.

I know there's a logic that I could use in my defense— "it was not my intention to harm" or "it's different because I'm a woman and there are imbalances of power" or "what about that boob joke in the season one *script*?" blah, etc., etc. So, sure, I could argue those defenses. But if I'm feeling the need to defend myself, that means I feel attacked. And I need to ask myself if what I'm perceiving as an attack is actually an attack. Who is the injured party here? They're the ones in need of defense. Not me. Sure, *I* think it's funny. Just because it's funny to me doesn't mean it has to be funny to everybody. My humor and my innocent intentions are not the standard that everyone must follow. And if someone else is hurt, rather than forcing my standard upon them to discredit their accusation, maybe I should just listen. Maybe I'll learn a standard that is different from mine. Maybe that's a good thing. So, when Justin talked to me about it, I listened.

I am writing this essay to get ahead of it and admit my guilt now. I apologize and recognize the problem. This is an earnest apology. From the bottom of my boob, I am sorry.

Driving a bumper car with E in back, 1990s

Pisha, Masha, and Me

It was the quietest part of my day. By the time I'd clocked out from the restaurant and gotten in my car it was often well past 2:00 a.m. The roads in LA are emptier at night, making the drive home smooth and easy. Exhausted from the long day, I'd pull into the driveway of my apartment building, turn off the car, and just sit there.

At that time, my car was a black Toyota Prius that I'd bought used. I spent my whole day in that car, driving to auditions all over LA, blasting the radio or mixed CDs that boys had made for me. Or I'd run my audition lines, mumbling them to myself over and over again until I knew them by heart. I'd do that all day. The relentless LA sunshine making my left arm several shades darker than my right. My last stop of the day was the restaurant where I waited tables. It was a high-pressure job—heat from the kitchen, demanding customers, plates and silverware constantly clanging. The quicker you turned your tables, the more money you made, so it was all hustle hustle hustle. (Sometimes I'd wake up in the middle of the night in a panic shouting, "Where's the vodka cranberry for table eleven?!") After the shift, I'd do my side work and cash out while commiserating with the waitstaff about the night. I usually ordered a glass of wine as my one free shift drink, and I needed it.

When I arrived home, I never went inside right away. I'd turn off the car so it got dark and quiet. I'd look up at the flickering light in my apartment window—my roommate watching TV. Exhausted from the long, loud day, I'd think about the comfort of my bed, mere steps away. I could have gone right up to my apartment to sleep in my bed or eat Lean Pockets with my roommate. Instead, I'd just sit in the car for a while. No music, just the light clicking sounds of the car settling. The street I lived on was wide and quiet, lined with a few palm trees. I remember the way those high palm leaves looked, their outlines illuminated by buzzing streetlamps and moonlight. This was before I had a smartphone, so I wasn't doing anything. I would just sit there and listen to the car settle. Sometimes I sat there for a very long time.

———

My first car was an '88 Chevy Corsica. I got it in 1998, my junior year of high school. My mom bought it off a friend for something ridiculously cheap, like five hundred dollars. It was a crap car. But since neither of my two older sisters had gotten cars when they turned sixteen, it was a big deal. My sisters may have resented the privilege, but the decision was a practical one—I did so many plays in high school that taking me to and from rehearsals every day was a pain for my parents. So they got me a car.

She was boxy and burgundy, inside and out. She had a black stripe that went around her exterior. Inside, she was upholstered in two types of burgundy fabric: thin-wale corduroy on the seats, and soft felt on the ceiling and sides. Over the years, the ceiling's adhesive wore off and the fabric began detaching in small bubbles that eventually combined into bigger bubbles, till finally the whole thing pillowed down from the ceiling, grazing the head of anyone tall.

One day, when I was driving around with a friend, we began mock lamenting about what a piece of crap my car was. Moaning dramatically, "Piece of crap! Piece of crap!" Somehow "piece of" started to sound like "pisha." And that's when we decided her full name. First name: Pisha. Last name: Crap.

Even my parents referred to her as Pisha. "Did you get the starter on Pisha fixed?" "Did Pisha pass inspection?" Of all the cars we ever had: the Mazda, the Corolla, the Mercury, the Mitsubishi . . . Pisha was the only car that my whole family referred to by name. She was like the family pet—a mangy ol' dog who was constantly at the vet.

She had so many problems. Her horn didn't work—so I had to be extra mindful of distracted drivers. Her headlights were tricky. They were controlled by a square button, but it was broken. When you pushed it down, it popped right back out. So if you were driving at night, you had to either hold the button down for the entire drive or have my magic touch—applying pressure at a certain angle and giving it a little jiggle to the right and the button stayed put! I was the only one in my family who could keep her lights on. She had a tiny leak in her oil tank, a slow one that completely emptied the tank every six to eight weeks, if you weren't careful. I learned how to check her oil level and quality, so I knew when to refill it. When the dipstick came up dry or low, I went to Pep Boys and bought a cheap plastic bottle of motor oil and refilled it myself, oblivious to how horrible it was for the environment.

Pisha broke down many times, and I learned something about cars each time. How to jump a battery, what the alternator did. She had to have her rotors replaced, her starter. I got to know her so well that I began to enjoy the maintenance. Listening for suspicious sounds and smells, laughing with my friends about how crappy she was. Driving a humble car made me feel *real*. I didn't want to be one of those lame rich kids with a Lexus. I preferred life with Pisha, where it was always an adventure. Where you never knew if she would start, or when she might quit.

And of course, she quit on what remains one of the scariest nights of my life. I was a senior in high school, working on a term paper. I had procrastinated, and it was due the next day. To avoid distractions at home, I went to VCU's twenty-four-hour library, using my dad's faculty pass to get in. I stayed there for hours, finishing around midnight. And as I was driving home that night, Pisha decided to quit. She just . . . stopped. In the middle of the road. Wouldn't start.

I was stranded downtown. There weren't cell phones back then so I couldn't call my parents or AAA. It was late at night, so nothing was open, and she'd broken down in a residential area, so there weren't any pay phones either.

Even if there had been, I didn't have any money. Not even a damn quarter. I didn't know anyone who lived nearby. It was too far and too dark to walk anywhere. I had no choice but to go knocking on strangers' doors in the middle of the night . . . in a neighborhood that was much rougher than the gentle suburbs I'd grown up in.

It is scary to knock on strangers' doors in the middle of the night, especially when you're a teenager. I tried one; no answer. Moving on to the next, where a thirty-something man opened the door. I attempted to explain, "I need to use your phone . . . my car . . . I can't . . ." unable to finish because I burst into tears. The man softened. "Oh, honey, of course you can. Come in, come in." He led me into his kitchen, where I called my mom. I was still crying hard, and I didn't know where I was, didn't know the address. "I . . . I don't know where I am!" I sobbed. In desperation, I handed the phone to the man. He took over, gave her directions to his house, assured her that I was safe. And then I had to wait, alone with a stranger, until my mom got there.

I felt embarrassed of my crying, but you know I can't stop my tears. The man tried to calm me down by showing me a photo album of his house. He had bought the house for next to nothing and had spent a year fixing it up. He showed me the before and after photos, talked about the antique furniture he had bought, and told me where he'd gotten each piece and why it was special to him. I looked at the pictures and listened to his stories and gradually stopped crying, asking him questions between hiccups.

When my mom finally arrived, I was ready to get the hell out of there—so embarrassed of the scene I had made—but my whimsical mom never passed up an opportunity to socialize. This was no exception. So she asked him about the flowers in his front yard and they began to chat gardening. He made her a cup of tea and they proceeded to talk about how to get your azaleas to bloom longer or whatever. Richmonders. I was annoyed, but glad my mom was there. Later, I wrote him a thank-you card and put it in the mail. I wish I remembered his name. I'm lucky the first person who opened the door was so nice.

When Pisha's tire blew up on the highway, I was driving home from my job at the local theme park, Paramount's Kings Dominion. I was driving full speed on I-64, when all of a sudden I heard a *POP* and a terrible clanking noise and the car started shaking. I pulled over to the side of the highway to find my rear right tire completely shredded. I started to panic—I didn't know how to change a tire! But within a minute, a young couple pulled over to check their own car. They had run over the hubcap that my blown tire had shed. While their car was fine, they saw me alone and came to check on me.

"Can you help me? What do I do?" I asked, panicked. They were a friendly, white, college-aged couple. They were glad to help. The guy took the spare out of the trunk. As he jacked the car up, I was so grateful for his help. . . . I never would have been able to do that by myself! He wrenched the bolts off Pisha's tire. Some of them were rusted so tight he had to stand on the tool to loosen them. As his girlfriend and

I watched, he talked us through it, teaching us so we would be prepared if either of us were ever alone and this happened again. He finished changing the tire and wiped his hands on his jeans. His girlfriend gave me a hug and wished me well.

"Just get it changed in the next couple days," he said. I thanked him profusely.

"Don't even worry about it," they said, smiling. "Glad to help."

Again, Richmonders—so friendly and caring.

My first year of college, I left Pisha at home. But my sophomore year, I drove her from Virginia to Upstate New York where she stuck with me for the remainder of college. We went through some harsh New York winters together and oh boy, she did *not* like it. She made horrendous noises, like if a car could have bronchitis, she had it. Her heat periodically broke, and when it did work it smelled weird. (And in the summertime, forget about the AC. She refused.) The burgundy paint on her hood started peeling in spots, revealing the silver metal underneath. I flaked off the edges when they began to curl because, like picking a scab, I couldn't resist. By the end of her first year in New York, her burgundy hood was speckled with bare metal spots, including one spot the size of a large pizza. I bought a cheap can of red spray paint and spray-painted all the bald spots. It dried a different color, making her hood resemble burgundy camouflage. She looked so ridiculous it kind of made me love her more.

Like a one-eyed bunny or a happy three-legged dog who is unbothered by his lost limb.

Whenever I felt sad or lost in college (which was a lot), I took Pisha out for late-night drives. I'd drive around in the dark listening to the radio show *Delilah*. People from all over the country called in and talked to Delilah about love and loneliness. The callers were often desperate or in denial. But Delilah was always warm. Her soothing alto voice was a comfort during those lonely late-night drives. After a while, I'd drive to the twenty-four-hour Stop & Shop, where I'd roam the fluorescent aisles, inspecting the calorie counts on boxes. I'd buy a bag of cinnamon apple chips, sit with Pisha in the parking lot, and eat the whole bag, licking the sugar off my fingers.

After college, I moved to Manhattan. I took Pisha along too. But after a couple months, the hassle of street parking proved to be too much. I knew it was time to let her go. I loved her, but I was a New Yorker now; I didn't need a car. I drove Pisha back to Virginia. Surprisingly, she had no problems on the drive down. On the last trip I ever took with her, she gave me an easy ride. It was like she was saying goodbye. *Thanks for taking care of me.* A few weeks later, she died at her original home in Virginia.

———

In New York, the only cars I ever rode in were cabs. Back when I lived there, cabs didn't have TV screens and cab fare was only paid in *cash*. No credit cards. Cabbies didn't make conversation and smartphones hadn't been invented yet. All

you had were your thoughts and the windows. I loved looking out cab windows at night. It was so dreamy to watch the
city whirring by and wondering about all the lives it held.
It moved me. But it wasn't the fancy/touristy places that
moved me. It was the plain stuff. The bodegas and Duane
Reades. The Citibanks with their fluorescent ATM alcoves.
Bars where patrons smoked outside. A closed newsstand
with its metal accordion shade drawn and locked. Gates
protecting darkened boutiques with shoes still glowing in
the display. I'd look at it all and marvel, *Wow, I live in New
York City.* Even when I had a bad day, looking out a cab
window at night still inspired awe. *Everything is terrible, but
this is where I get to live.* I'd dreamed of it my whole life.

One summer night, I fell apart in a cab. I was twenty years
old, and my boyfriend and I got into a fight. I was working
as an usher at a theater when he called me, drunk, picked a
fight, and demanded I come home. As I stumbled outside, the
streets blurred with people and the sounds of the city blared
in my ears. He'd said some vicious, cruel things to me, and a
piercing pain was rising in my chest. I held it off while I hailed
a cab, didn't want anyone to see me crying. A taxi pulled up,
and I got in, shut the door, barely choked out my destination
to the driver. He nodded and started driving, and that's when
I finally let myself cry. It was ugly—hyperventilating between
sobs, it was the kind of crying you do only in private. For
New Yorkers, being in a cab is like being alone. Other than
establishing destinations and routes, the passenger and the
cabdriver don't acknowledge each other's presence. It sounds

cold, but that's just the way it is. Crying, making out, arguing, you name it—all that stuff was normal in an NYC cab. (Years later, when I was living in LA, my then boyfriend thought it was rude that I didn't engage in small talk with Uber drivers, and I thought it was weird that *he* chatted with *them*.)

That entire cab ride, I couldn't stop crying. The cabdriver didn't seem to pay me any mind, and I didn't acknowledge his presence—the way it always was. So, when the cabbie pulled over, I was surprised. He glanced in the rearview mirror, held up a finger, and said, "Just one minute," before dashing into a bodega, leaving me confused in the backseat. He even left the cab running. He came out a moment later carrying a plastic bag that he handed me without a word. He got back in the driver's seat and continued being a silent, invisible NYC cabdriver. I looked in the bag. He had bought me a box of Kleenex and a bottle of water. I even remember the brand of water: it was Fiji.

Whenever I tell this story, people always assume that he did all of this in a warm, caring manner. Sometimes dudes accuse him of having an ulterior motive. They're wrong. He wasn't warm. He was brusque. Efficient. He didn't try to soothe me or cheer me up. He didn't seek any acknowledgment for the tissues/water. He didn't ask me what was wrong; he didn't check on me in the rearview mirror. More than the water, more than the tissues, it was his coarseness that felt the most caring. He allowed me the privacy of being alone with my feelings. Of not having to explain myself. There is dignity in the anonymity of NYC cabs. He just got me tissues and let me cry.

When we got to my apartment, I tried to pay him back for the water and tissues. But he wouldn't accept anything, not even the cab fare (and it had been a long cab ride, from downtown up to Ninety-Ninth Street—a substantial cost). He refused it all, saying, "No, no. It's okay," and drove off. I never even got his name.

———————

Years later, I moved to LA, where a car was a necessity. I bought an old red Ford Taurus off Craigslist for a thousand dollars cash. When I picked it up, the guy had it running already. He took the cash and I drove away. On the way home, I stopped at a 7-Eleven to buy a soda, and when I came back, the car wouldn't start. I'd owned it for five minutes, and it was already dead! I called the guy who sold it to me. He apologized, acted confused, and brought some jumper cables to the 7-Eleven to help me. He jumped the car and instructed me to drive it around for a bit. Pisha had had plenty of battery and alternator problems, so I understood. He gave me the jumper cables as a gift. Probably as an apology for selling me a lemon. I could have accused him of selling me a shit car, but I didn't because I worried it might hurt his feelings. And I didn't want to seem like I was "difficult." Instead, I smiled, thanked him, and drove away in what ended up being the worst car I ever owned.

That car sucked and I only had it for a few months. Not long enough to even give it a name. There was no Uber or Lyft back then, and I was carless in LA for a bit. When I got the check for a commercial I'd done a few weeks prior, I walked to a used Toyota dealership a few blocks from my apartment. I test-drove *one* car at random, thought, *Eh, this'll be fine.* (Pisha had taught me not to be vain about my car.) But I was forty thousand dollars in credit card debt and was worried I wouldn't be approved for financing. Turns out I was a GREAT candidate for financing because I always paid my bills on time, even if I only ever paid the minimum. I've always been terrible at haggling—I can't tolerate the discomfort. So I think I asked for only, like, fifty dollars off the sticker price. The car salesman came back in two seconds and said, "My manager was in a good mood; he approved your offer! You got quite a steal!" My heart sank as I realized I'd been ripped off, and it was my own fault. Oh well!

That ended up being a great car. It was a black 2007 Certified Pre-Owned Toyota Prius. By the time I got her, she was already three years old. I named her Masha, after the character in Chekhov's *The Seagull* who "always wore black." Masha never had any major problems, except once when her catalytic converter was stolen while I was away for Thanksgiving, but that wasn't her fault.

I spent a lot of time alone in that car. When I drove to studio auditions, I arrived early so I could sit in the parking garage doing my makeup in the mirror and going over my audition lines. When I returned from the audition, I'd sit in the car and mope. There's this sinking feeling you get when you give your whole heart at an audition but know that you didn't get the part. That even at your best they don't want you.

Masha and I took lots of road trips together: A weekend in Ojai with a guy I was madly in love with for about three weeks. Tahoe with my best friend Jeff, for his cousin's wedding. Utah for the Sundance Labs, my pet bunny tagging along in the backseat. Many drives to Palm Springs with my friends— we love going there. Love getting out of the city, stopping by Starbucks halfway for coffee and peeing. As you get closer to Palm Springs, there are enormous power windmills you can see from the freeway. They look like Mercedes signs. Blue sky, tan desert, and white Mercedes emblems spinning like pinwheels.

In 2014, I started to enjoy some success thanks to *Fresh Off the Boat*. I was finally out of debt and had surplus money for the first time in my life. But even then, I refused to buy a new car. I wasn't going to abandon Masha; she was my badge of honor. Just like Pisha had made me feel more down-to-earth than the snobby rich kids I'd always judged, Masha represented my refusal to let fame change me. Back then, my success always felt like an illusion. Like I'd eventually return to who I was before it—the scrappy kid with a scrappy car to match. Sometimes, I even joked that Masha was Pisha, reincarnated. It would be years before I even *considered* buying a new car.

––––––––––

I ended up sticking with Masha for almost nine years.

One day, during a routine inspection, I was told that she required a repair that cost significantly more than her value. I got quiet when the mechanic told me the news, nodding with resignation. Masha had been with me since before I was famous. She'd helped me *get* there, ridden me *through* it. And now she was telling me it was time to put her down.

Then the mechanic said he was a fan of my TV show and asked if he could take a selfie with me. "Sure," I said as he fumbled with his phone.

A month later, I got a white Mercedes plug-in electric hybrid. It has tinted windows, a touch screen, and a sunroof. When you put your seatbelt on, it hugs you back. I named her Blanche DuBois, after *Streetcar*. But that name hasn't really stuck. This car just feels like a car. It's not Masha and it's definitely not Pisha. Maybe it's because she's a lease. She works great but one thing that bothers me is that her radio doesn't turn off with the ignition; it only turns off when you open the door. Pisha and Masha weren't like that. Sometimes, I'll open the door and then shut it, so I can enjoy some quiet. But it's not the same as those late nights after a waitressing shift when I'd sit alone in a quiet car.

In the years between Masha and the Mercedes, smartphones became ubiquitous. Whereas it was once considered rude to check your phone during a meal, iPhones now have a proverbial seat at the table. They're active participants during meals—they fact-check a heated topic of conversation, they take notes and coordinate schedules, their cameras commemorate the moment. Maybe I'm old-fashioned, but it's depressing to see people on their phones at group dinners. Or single men at bars, not talking to the bartender or to each other, but hunched over their phones, swiping. Or folks waiting in checkout lines, mindlessly browsing social media. Just as I had resisted other markers of success—hiring a cleaning person, having a nice car—I resisted smartphones for a long time too. I preferred keeping a flip phone that made calls and texts via a number pad. But eventually, I needed to be able to check email on my phone, and I switched over too.

Getting an iPhone kinda felt like giving up an old beater for a fancy new car. I have mixed feelings about it. I'd like to say that I'm still the same person I was pre-iPhone, pre-success. The person who drove around listening to Delilah, who stared out the window of a New York City cab, who spray-painted her piece-a-crap car's hood the wrong color and loved her the more for it. That I am still the person who enjoys being alone in cars. But everything is different these days. Sometimes I still sit alone in the car when I get home, but I'm usually scrolling my phone when I do. When I'm in taxi cabs, I always turn off the screen so I can stare out the windows, but it's not dreamy like it used to be—even in a taxi with the screen turned off, it takes a conscious effort to keep my hands and eyes from wandering to my phone. It often happens before I've even realized it, and I'm always disappointed in myself when it does.

I know tirades against phone addiction and social media have become as commonplace as phones themselves. I don't know why I try. I can't upend an entire cultural shift, just like I can't pretend that fame hasn't changed my life. But I can remember the cars I had, and who I was when I had them. Back when I could be alone in a car, after a long night of waiting tables in the city where I was pursuing my dreams. Sitting in the quiet, doing nothing. Listening to the car settle.

Posing for Dad in the Shenandoah Valley

Unfinished Mansions

It was after both of my older sisters went to college, when my mom started breaking us into houses. Our family lived in a quaint, quiet part of town—a place where your neighbors made you pies, where there were more churches than road signs. But it was starting to change. Woods were being cleared, and new subdivisions were springing up. The newest one was near us, and it was all mansions. Glorious estates sprawled among rolling green hills, edged by lush forests. Each mansion was unique. Some had tennis courts or their own private ponds. One had a huge copper dome that stood atop towering pillars over the front door. They were all under construction, so no one lived there yet and my mom discovered that they were empty on the weekends. So, on Sundays, she took me and my little sister, E, to explore these huge unfinished mansions.

Most of the doors didn't even have locks yet, so we didn't really break in per se, we just sort of . . . walked in. If the front somehow was locked, Mom always found a way. Through the sliding glass doors out back or an unlocked bay window. Maybe the side door of the garage. Curious and unafraid, we'd climb in and breathe the New House Smell. Fragrant, fine sawdust the color of cake batter covered the floors. The smell of fresh paint and new appliances. Milky-white plastic tarps thrown over banisters and cabinets. The windows, under their plastic Pella film, had never seen a fingerprint.

Mom walked E and me through the houses, pointing things out, teaching us. "This is called a lazy Susan"; "That's a slate roof—sturdy and beautiful"; "A lovely sunken living room!"; "That copper dome is shiny orange now, but it will turn bright green one day. Just like the Statue of Liberty." She instructed us to pretend we were living there—asking us which rooms we wanted and why.

"I like this one because of the windows," E offered.

"This one is mine because of the walk-in closet!" I said.

She asked us where we'd put our beds, what color curtains we wanted. If there would be carpets and what they'd look like.

"Where should we put your piano?" Mom asked me, her only musical daughter.

Playing pretend life in these mansions was intoxicating. E and I ran from room to room, up and down stairways like kings or animals, our shouts and squeals echoing through the empty hallways. The open space and possibility of it all made us wild. But for Mom, it was calming. Gliding through those mansions, she'd smile as she watched over us—the youngest of her four daughters—with a love so beautifully plain. I remember the houses with huge floor-to-ceiling windows—Mom's peaceful smile when she gazed out of them at the lush green hills lined by stone-gray sky that looked like how cold feels, or how I imagined Ireland. Sometimes she stayed there for a long time, looking out the windows, the shouts and flopping footsteps of her daughters echoing from distant parts of the house. When we returned to her, flushed and out of breath, she'd still be staring out the window.

Mom grew up in Taipei, the daughter of a doctor and a homemaker. I loved listening to her stories of being a young girl because she was the kind of girl I wanted to be. Pretty, popular, at ease with herself. As a child, I worshipped beauty and Mom was *so* beautiful . . . the most beautiful girl at her school in Taipei, my relatives often told me. But it felt like she was the most beautiful woman in Richmond too. When my fifth-grade teacher, Mrs. Murray, met my mom during a parent-teacher conference, she singled me out the next day in front of the whole class and proclaimed, "Your mom is so *beautiful*." She shook her head, her eyes widening with impossibility as though my mom's beauty was a grave discovery. She didn't say anything about any of the other moms and I felt proud. Proud that Mom was beautiful not just to Asian people but to *everyone*, including Mrs. Murray, a blond Southern lady who said "y'all." Asian American girls who grew up in white neighborhoods in the South during the eighties and early nineties will understand why that's a big deal. Growing up in those neighborhoods, "pretty" always meant blond hair and blue eyes and boobs.

Mom was flat-chested and lean. She had black hair and dark eyes, and her skin was bright and clear. She walked with a dancer's elegance. Her only flaw was a raised scar the size of a matchbox on her left shoulder—a reaction from a childhood smallpox vaccine. She often tried covering that scar, but I thought it made her long, slender arms look even more beautiful. Like Cindy Crawford's mole, it was the type of flaw that took conventional prettiness and transformed it into a beauty that ached.

Mom took care of herself—wore beautiful, understated makeup, dressed well. Around the time she met Mrs. Murray, she was wearing these wide, flat grosgrain ribbon clips in her hair. She placed them perfectly at the nape of her long neck, pinning back her shiny black ponytail. The ribbon clips always complemented her dresses—tea-length printed dresses with shoulder pads and cinched waists in drapey fabrics that swung with her body just right. Mom was frugal and never owned expensive jewelry. But the cheap jewelry she *did* own—enamel earrings or plated necklaces from JCPenney—was always the perfect touch. The effect was elegant.

She had brains too! As a teenager in Taiwan, she'd gone to a school called the Number One Girls High School. She'd show my little sister and me pictures of the school and beam. "You had to take a test to get in," she boasted, her eyes gleaming with a fixed pride, as if somewhere in those old sepia photographs was an accomplishment that no one could ever take away from her.

In most of her old photographs she had a closed-mouth smile . . . because when she was a kid, open-mouthed smiles weren't considered appropriate for photographs. But her real-life smile was joyful and bright. It could light up a room; so could her laugh, and she laughed often back then. She had a unique ability to find delight in contrary opinions. It made her easy to love. At church choir rehearsals, the WASP-y church ladies always asked after her, told me how much they loved her. Our elderly next-door neighbors Betty and Syd loved her. All the community theater moms visibly brightened whenever she came to one of my rehearsals. Mom had the kind of charm you can't teach. When I imagine her as a teenager, she's Penny Lane from *Almost Famous* floating into a party—the entire room cheering upon her arrival. Penny Lane, the girl that every boy was in love with. Penny Lane, barefoot on the empty dance floor, a tiny dancer twirling on confetti.

Mom loved to dance. As a child, she'd been a ballerina. She often bragged about being selected for *Swan Lake*'s *danse des petits cygnes*. "It's really hard," she'd say as she demonstrated a plié for me and my little sister. "You have to match the other three ballerinas exactly." Her long arm arched over her head, effortless, index finger slightly raised above the rest. In our living room we used a banister as a barre. Mom put mirrors up on the wall and tried to teach us ballet. E and I were terrible dancers, but she didn't care if we were good or not. She just liked to watch her daughters dance. "This is first position, and this is second. And you have to squeeze your butt in all of the positions!" she exclaimed, making me and E giggle. Then the three of us would dance around the room together, squeezing our butts. She'd show us a pirouette, and we'd fall over trying to copy her.

The pirouetting sometimes turned into a game that E and I invented—a "space travel" game where we spun around and around so fast until we became dizzy and collapsed on the floor, limbs splayed out like starfish. With our eyes squeezed shut and our heads spinning like crazy, shouting, "I'm flying to Brazil! I am in France! I am on Mars! I am on a farm with many chickens!" Somehow, we equated dizziness with space travel. Mom loved that we played together so well. Our two older sisters often fought with each other, but me and E were best friends like she and her sister had been. Our aunt Mona.

As kids, she and Mona went to the same noodle shack next to their school every day, where they got a snack of live mini-shrimp. The bowl came with a sealable lid because the shrimp jumped out if you didn't keep the lid on between bites. E and I shrieked when we heard this story.

"No way!" we exclaimed.

"Yes way!" Mom said, nodding with grave authority.

"Ewwww grossss!!!!" we'd scream as we ran around the room, collapsing on the floor in giggles.

Mom took pleasure in making things with her hands. An excellent cook, she made dinner every night. White rice was a staple—we always had a giant economy-sized sack of rice and kept the rice cooker running. My favorite food she made was Japanese chicken curry. I always knew when she started cooking it, because I could smell the onions browning in the skillet. I'd bound downstairs to watch her simmer the onions, listening to their sizzle, salivating as she added seared chicken, potatoes, and carrots. It was all stirred into the yellow Japanese curry sauce, and then sealed into a pressure cooker. It made the house smell wonderful. When it was ready, I'd put a huge scoop of rice on my plate and pour the curry stew all over it.

Mom always set the Morton Salt container by my plate because she knew I added a ton of salt. It was salty enough for everyone else in my family, but not me. I liked a lot of salt.

She kept our kitchen cabinets stocked with boxes of Duncan Hines cake mixes that we baked together on weekends. She could crack an egg with one hand and scrape batter from the bowl in one clean spatula swipe. We had a hand mixer and two cake pans—a thirteen-by-nine cake tin so old it was a black type of brown and a newer Bundt pan that we used for marble cakes. I remember eating cake straight out of the oven, still so hot that steam rose out of it as Mom sliced. I liked the corner pieces best.

She taught us how to sew. E was always bored by it, but I loved using the sewing machine—pressing the pedal, threading the bobbin, cutting the thread on the razor behind the needle, going back and forth to close the end of a seam. When I wanted to make my own costume for my high school production of *Grease*, Mom took me to Jo-Ann to choose a pattern and fabric. I knew the basics, having sewed pillowcases with her. But Mom taught me how to sew from a pattern—to pin the thin brown tissue pattern on the fabric and cut it to size, running a spiked wheel thing over chalk paper to mark up the fabric with a dotted line. It took several weeks, but I finished it all by myself! I was very proud of that dress.

She often took us to Maymont Park. E and I loved it because there was a petting zoo and huge green hills that we rolled down like logs, racing each other. Mom loved the Japanese Garden. Lush and serene, it had a large stepping-stone pond. We'd walk over the cement circles on the pond, pointing at koi fish. Or sit in the gazebo eating Pocky while mom taught us about flowers.

"That is a chrysanthemum," she'd say. "You have to pinch off the small buds so that bigger blooms will grow. You'll get bigger flowers." She loved gardening and wanted us to love it, too. There was a plant nursery on the Southside she took us to once, treating us each to one plant of our choice. E chose purple pansies, and I got pink impatiens. Mom got an African violet. But gardening never stuck for us. I was too afraid of bugs and worms. E killed every plant she ever owned.

And then there were the ducks.

During fall in Richmond, the leaves turned bright orange and red, almost fluorescent when the sun hit them. Mom often took us to the nearby University of Richmond to enjoy the fall colors and feed the ducks. U of R was a beautiful school—old buildings and tall trees and a lake in the middle of campus. The air by that lake was the good kind of cold—it made your cheeks rosy and revitalized your lungs. Oh, how we loved those ducks! We brought stale bread to feed them. There was one very special duck—he was a funny duck because he was different from the others. He had puffy feathers that stuck out of his head, like a bouffant. Mom named him Kramer (she loved *Seinfeld* and laughed so hard whenever Kramer slid into Jerry's apartment). When we got to the lake, E and I would rush down from the parking lot to see who could find Kramer first! We'd try to give him the best, softest parts of the bread.

After we fed the ducks, Mom took us to the student commons to warm up. At the end of the lake, the commons was a large stone building with humongous windows that spanned the height of the building. Mom would treat me and E to something to share from the vending machine as she helped herself to the free coffee that was on a burner plate. Sitting on the sofas, she watched over us as we sat on the floor right up against the windows overlooking the lake, our noses pressed to the tinted glass. "Look, Mom, I see Kramer!" We would point and wiggle as we licked potato chip salt off our fingers.

Mom's Taiwanese peers often ask her how she raised me to become so successful and her answer has always been: "I didn't do anything! I just let her do whatever she wanted." Her style of parenting was hands-off; she never pressured me. Mom wasn't a tiger mom or even a stage mom. She was Penny Lane! So, while there was cake baking, trips to Maymont, gardening, and breaking into mansions, there were never any SAT classes, no making me do homework (which is why I often didn't). She let me do as I pleased, and I was always the one who took initiative—begging for piano lessons or theater auditions. So long as it was wholesome and I was happy, she was supportive. The *Richmond Times-Dispatch* had a weekly section that listed local theater auditions. I waited all week for that section of the paper, running to my parents whenever I found one: "Mom, see! They're looking for kids my age for this show! Can I go, please? Pretty, pretty, please?" Dad took me to Boykin's to buy sheet music for an audition song. And Mom drove me downtown to the auditions, waiting in the lobby while I belted out my sixteen bars. Even back then, theater consumed me. If I wasn't at acting class or play rehearsal or chorus practice, I was counting the hours till I would be there.

I had been acting in community theater for a couple years when my middle school drama teacher, Mr. Frizzell, handed me a flyer advertising a local casting call for a movie. They were looking for middle school kids! The flyer listed

a hotline you could call to schedule an audition. As soon
as I got home, I called the hotline, but all the audition slots
were full. "Sorry," the lady on the phone said. I had gotten
the flyer too late. I hung up, threw away the flyer, and cried.
I was so upset.

One Saturday morning, several weeks later, Mom
knocked on my door and asked me to come with her to drop
off my big sister at her weekend retail job at the mall. I was
groggy, didn't want to go.

"We'll go to Applebee's after," she said. "I'll get you a
Belgian waffle with whipped cream and strawberries."

Sold! I got ready sloppily, but Mom said, "Dress nicer,"
which was weird for her to say, because neither of my
parents ever cared what their daughters wore. Seeing my
confusion, she clarified, "Dress nicer because we are going
to Applebee's." I changed into a pretty floral skirt and light
purple T-shirt from Limited Too. After dropping my big sister
off, we went to Applebee's. As I devoured my humongous
whipped-cream-and-strawberry waffle, a quiet smile started
rising on Mom's face, even as she tried to hold it back—she
didn't want to spoil the surprise she had for me. As we left
the mall parking lot, she turned onto the highway.

"Where are we going?" I asked.

"You'll see," she said.

Thirty minutes later, we arrived at an unfamiliar building
where I saw a bunch of kids my age lined up outside.

It was the movie audition.

Mom had secretly called the hotline and charmed her

way into getting me an audition. Refused to give up until they squeezed me in. "Ta-da! I wanted to surprise you!" she exclaimed.

I was so happy I shrieked! It was the best surprise. I had a great audition, and I got a part in the movie. "Of course you did!" Mom said, proud. It wasn't really a movie—more like an educational video for the local public school system—but I was twelve years old, and it felt so fancy to me. I wouldn't have gotten it if it hadn't been for Mom. It wasn't because she wanted me to be an actress; she just wanted me to be happy. For her, that was all that mattered. We could play in the dirt, wear rags, not bathe, skip homework, eat crap—so long as we were happy, that's what she cared about.

Dad was the one who took our health very seriously. The slightest ailment and Dad took me to the doctor, even when I was a nineteen-year-old adult. While he was usually thrifty, when it came to medical care, the cost didn't matter. He researched the best doctors in the area, checking their credentials. He came to all my appointments, asking the doctor tons of questions and writing down every detail to compare it later with his own research. And this was all before the internet, so it's not like he could WebMD it—he had to do the *work* of research. Like, from the library. In both the surgeries I had (wisdom teeth and tonsil/adenoid removal) he missed work to take me and insisted on staying in the room the whole time. He was worried about me going under. I remember his face when I woke up from anesthesia. Sitting in the corner, hand over his mouth, softening with relief to see me awake.

Dad knew how to kill a spider. "Oh my GOD!!! Dad Dad DAD! SPIDER!" E and I would scream from our shared room. Not two seconds later, he'd stride in with a rubber band and a smile, squinting one eye as he took aim and shot the spider dead from across the room. We were always impressed, no matter how many times he did it. He'd grin at us as we jumped up onto the furniture shouting, "Eww, Dad, pick it up! Pick it up!" as though being on the same floor as the now-dead spider was the same as catching cooties. He'd grab a tissue and pick it up, making the room safe again. Sometimes he'd pretend scare us—chasing us around the room with the tissue, laughing as he threatened to rub the spider guts on us as we squealed.

Dad's origins were very different from Mom's. Though they were both from Taiwan, Mom was a city girl. Dad was from a humble farming family in a village so remote that his birth wasn't officially recorded until he was already several months old, because you had to travel into the city to register a birth, and the city was far and costly to get to. (He still doesn't know his real birthday.) He was the second oldest child in his family of five boys and one girl. They lived on a mountain in a small shack of a house with a tin roof. They had a farm with bamboo, mangoes, sweet potatoes, sugarcane, lychee trees. His father was a hard worker who had two jobs—he was both a local policeman *and* a farmer. Because both of those jobs were full-time, my dad and his brothers helped out on the farm. It was a family obligation. Dad often told us stories about him and his elder brother carrying sacks of pig manure on their backs for miles to fertilize the fields.

Sometimes, he skipped out on his farm chores and hid in the school's utility closets, where he sat and studied textbooks. His dad always spanked him for it—the farm was supposed to take precedence. But Dad was so passionate about science that, for him, it was worth it. The spankings stopped when he attended Taiwan's Provincial Normal School, a government-supported high school that trained its students to teach elementary school. Because students were required to live in barracks-style dorms for three years, he was no longer punished for studying. "I got to study, uninterrupted! That was freedom," he told us, as though it were a miracle. Education was such a joy to him. When he graduated at eighteen, he was placed in charge of teaching kids who were only five or six years younger than he was. He handed over all of his earnings to his parents. He went on to earn his bachelor's and master's degrees in Taiwan. Then his PhD in America, all on scholarship. He was still a poor, struggling graduate student when he married my mother.

I didn't know the story of my parents until I was in my early twenties, after they had been divorced for a few years. During a long car ride, I ventured to ask my dad how they had met. I had never asked either parent before. In my family there was an unspoken understanding that we weren't supposed to.

I've seen my dad cry three times. The first was when his father passed away. "My daddy died," he said one day when

I walked into his room. He got up from his chair, sniffling, and started organizing the VHS tapes on the shelf, avoiding eye contact. The way he said "daddy," like a small child, was crushing. I'd never heard him refer to his father that way. The second time I saw him cry was when he said goodbye to me and E before leaving on a long trip for a research sabbatical. She and I usually walked to the schoolbus stop, but Dad insisted on driving us that morning. Instead of dropping us off, he waited with us in the car, choking up when he saw the bus coming up the street. "Okay, bye-bye," he chirped, putting on a bright smile that looked somehow broken. And the third time I saw my dad cry was when he told me the story of marrying my mom.

She was working as an assistant across from his lab in Taiwan. "She was the most beautiful and charming girl," he said, his voice a strange combination of hurt and warning. "I fell in love with her. But she didn't pay much attention to me; she was so popular. And then I had to go away." He had gotten a full-ride scholarship at Michigan State's doctoral program. But he didn't forget her. "I wrote her letters almost every week. Every week for a whole year!" She didn't write a single letter back. Until one day, out of the blue, he got a letter from her. "We should get married," it said. "Come get me in Taipei and I will marry you."

He couldn't believe it. The girl he had been in love with for more than a year, the girl who had ignored every letter, the most charming and beautiful girl he'd ever met, was suddenly asking him, the poor, short science nerd, to marry her?

He had been happy to even get a *letter*! And to have it say that? He was beside himself.

He begged his adviser for time off to fly to Taiwan to marry my mother. "It was hard for me to ask for that," he said. "I was scared." He was in America on a scholarship and student visa and constantly worried that he could be kicked out at any moment and lose everything he'd worked for.

The professor, amused with his lovesick pupil, good-naturedly teased him by warning, "Okay, you can go . . . but this had better be the real thing." And with that, my dad flew back to Taiwan to marry my mother.

When he got there, he said, my mom was cold and blunt. "I don't know why I wrote that to you. I don't love you. I won't ever love you," she said. After he flew across the world full of hope and love and anticipation, *"I won't ever love you"* was what my mom said to him.

"But I still married her, because you know what? I was in love with her, even if she wasn't in love with me," Dad continued, eyes glued to the road. They got married. Dad flew back to America alone and my mom would follow in a month after sorting out moving and visa logistics. He told me that he was weeping so much on the flight back that the flight attendants were worried about him. "I decided on that flight that I was going to do whatever it took to earn her love," he told me. He had earned everything else in his life; he was determined to earn this too.

Later, when I tried to imagine what my mom had been thinking, I thought of my own moments of impulsiveness. The times when, overcome with emotion, I became reckless, desperate. It was almost always over a boy. I do the same thing after every heartbreak: First, I convince myself that I need to change something—my career, address, hairstyle. Next, my mind shuffles through a Rolodex of possible men. I select the safest one and call him on the phone. Speaking in a glib, upbeat tone in hopes of seeming attractive and easy-going. Every apartment move I've made has been initiated by a breakup. Unable to bear living in the same rooms I'd loved in, I've lived in many New York neighborhoods: two different apartments on the Upper East Side, the East Village, Washington Heights, Bushwick.

When George broke up with me, I was so heartbroken I didn't just move apartments; I moved across the damn country. Even though I was a diehard New Yorker, I just couldn't be in the city anymore—I got painful pangs in my chest whenever I saw a tall, lanky boy, a happy couple, a pretty girl. Weeping over my laptop, I booked my one-way ticket to LA, a place I'd sworn I'd never live. It was so impulsive that I booked it for the wrong date. Meant to book it for January 3 but accidentally booked it for December 3. I wouldn't realize the error until December 2, when I got an email to check in for my flight. I ended up having to pay for that flight twice.

Did that happen to my mom too? Did she have a George? Maybe he'd broken her heart so bad that she had to get away. Had she gone through her mental Rolodex of possible men, and my father seemed the safest bet? Maybe *that's* why she impulsively wrote him a proposal letter. He was the guy who was farthest away from her heartbreak, and he worshipped her. Maybe she was so desperate for anything to distract her from the pain of heartache, she wrote the letter to my dad and threw it in the mailbox without thinking, crying as she wandered the streets in a haze of despair. Maybe she even forgot she wrote it, so rash had it been. And when my dad arrived at her doorstep, his hopeful face filled her with guilt and shame—embarrassed of her impulsivity and even more embarrassed that he had actually shown up. Maybe she was too proud to admit it. Maybe she only said "I will never love you" to him to try to get him to change his mind and save both of them from making a decision they didn't fully understand. Maybe it was too hard or too late to admit her mistake. Maybe it was easier to just go along with it. It'd been her idea, after all. Maybe she thought it would make her ex-boyfriend jealous. Maybe, maybe, maybe. I didn't think I'd ever know why, because when I asked her about the letter, she got angry at me.

"How did you know that?" she demanded.

"Dad told me," I replied, turning red.

She left the room without answering.

———

I remember the day when Mom realized that she had passed a halfway mark. "*Huh*," she said, a faraway look in her eyes. "I've now lived in America for longer than I ever lived in

Taiwan." She seemed surprised, as though someone died so long ago that she was no longer grieving but she'd only just realized that she'd forgotten to attend the funeral. Like it had merely slipped her mind.

One day Mom picked me up from school and said she had been at the hospital earlier, "to get my tubes tied!" she announced with a snort. It was loud and sudden, her smile a mixture of indifference and mirth. A strange, harsh mirth that felt forced, like the squawk of a bird being squeezed.

"What does getting your tubes tied mean?" I asked.

She told me.

"Your dad made me do it! He refused to get snipped, even though it's easier, haha!"

I had never heard a laugh sound so bitter.

As the last of her four girls grew up, Mom decided it was time to go back to school. My two older sisters had left for and graduated from college. I was never home—always at play rehearsal or working my part-time bakery job at Montana Gold. E had retreated to spending entire weekends on the computer. Mom enrolled in night classes at a local community college and earned her degree in computer programming. Then she got a full-time job at city hall and didn't have time to be a homemaker anymore. That's when things started to change.

You don't notice change when it's gradual. But looking back, I can see the signs. When did she stop dressing beautifully? When was her charming smile replaced with a furrowed frown? She used to be such a social butterfly, but when did she stop going to church potlucks with all the blond Southern ladies? Her laughter, once so frequent and joyous, was becoming rarer and rarer. Sometimes, even spiteful.

Without mom at the helm, our house fell apart. The dishes piled up, spilling over until E or I got so grossed out we'd do them. The bathroom tub darkened with mildew, and the drain clogged—sometimes taking an entire day to drain. Mom stopped doing laundry, saying, "You're big enough to do it yourself." We whined about the house, as though it was all her fault. She often forgot to pick me up from play rehearsal, complaining about spending her life as a chauffeur, resenting the expectation. I'd call Marrianne in tears, asking her if she could pick me up. It was embarrassing, having to ask someone else to take me home, making up excuses for Mom because I was too ashamed to say *she forgot me.*

She stopped cooking chicken curry or thousand-year-old egg tofu for dinner. Instead, she stuck frozen fish sticks in the toaster oven. Handed my sister a box of powdered mashed potatoes to make herself. Or took us to Arby's for Beef 'n Cheddars and curly fries. My last couple years at home, we had pizza delivered a lot. My dad complained, but it didn't bother E and me.

She started making more money than Dad, and they began arguing a lot. My dad, having been the breadwinner for so long, became resentful and angry. He wanted her to contribute more. She reacted with paranoia and possessiveness. This was *her* money, she had *earned* it, she'd cry.

She became obsessed with the stock market. Without Dad's knowledge, she took all of E's and my college savings and invested it in one stock, which quickly plummeted to a fraction of its original value. More arguing and blame followed, and she reacted with churlishness and defiance.

She spontaneously flew off on a European vacation. While she was in Europe, my dad had to try being a single parent for the first time in his life. E and I were teenagers, so it wasn't that bad, but he didn't have any preparation or guidance. When he tried to cook dinner, he consulted an actual cookbook, something I'd never seen either of my parents do. He was trying to make us something really good—I think it was tempura something. As he went back and forth between the stove and the cookbook, his hands covered in flour, brow sweating, his face full of worry, I felt guilty.

Other than about money, I only recall them having one big fight. It was over a small thing. Dad was in the habit of going to sleep earlier than Mom. When Mom came in later, she put lotion on her hands and feet before bed. The squeezing of the lotion bottle was noisy and woke Dad up. He asked her to put the lotion on in the bathroom instead, because of the noise. I don't know how it escalated; all I remember is their screaming. Dad never raised his voice. E and I, too terrified to make eye contact, lingered near each other for safety, feeling quiet and small. Later, after Dad stormed out of the room, I saw Mom on her hands and knees, crying as she tried to scrape up lotion that had spilled all over the carpet.

After that, Mom moved into a different bedroom. The lotion bottle noise that woke my dad up was replaced by Mom walking around the attic at 2:00 or 3:00 a.m. Vacuuming or rearranging. Moving boxes, looking for something. It woke all of us up.

My friend Jack once told me about the time he traveled alone with his nine-month-old baby on an airplane. So many strangers came up to him in the airport, asking if he needed help, commending him for being such a great dad, alone with his baby, like he was a hero. How many mothers were on their own at that airport traveling with kids? Where were their medals? When my dad had to be a single father for *one week* during my mom's European vacation, I felt so bad for him. But where was that sympathy for my mom when she had to be a single mother for *months* while Dad was on his research sabbatical?

I used to judge my mom, but looking back I realize how unfair we all were to her.

We complained when she stopped doing the housework and cooking, insensitive to the fact that she had a full-time job and oblivious to the sexism of our gendered housekeeping expectations. While her daughters were pursuing their dreams, we expected her to stay the same and became indignant when she didn't. She'd spent so much of her life giving us space to blossom. We never thought about whether she might want to blossom too.

———————

One day, when E and I were both in high school, Dad's gallbladder burst. It happened late at night, after a big pizza dinner, when E and I were already asleep. The next morning, while he was in surgery, Mom didn't tell us and we went to school like it was any other morning. Later that afternoon, Mom took us to the hospital without explanation and dropped us off in our dad's recovery room. It was scary to see Dad in a hospital gown. It pained him to see us so quiet; he knew quiet meant scared. He tried hard to smile. "It doesn't hurt anymore," he reassured us. "You don't even need a gallbladder!"

There in that hospital room, I felt something change. My dad would later reveal to me that that was the night he realized he had to leave my mom. He had been in so much pain when his gallbladder burst, but Mom refused to take him to the hospital, complaining again about her life spent as a chauffeur. But dad's doctor said it was life-threatening and told him to go to the ER immediately. In too much pain to drive himself, he almost had to call an ambulance. "Your mom didn't want to take me to the hospital because she didn't think it was a big deal," he said, upset. "She wanted me to beg." In the end she drove him to the ER only because she worried about the cost of an ambulance. "That's when I knew," he sighed, his face filled with heartbreak, "I knew that she'd never take care of me."

A few months later, I was headed to college in New York. Mom and I packed into her Mercury Mystique for the seven-hour drive. She stayed the night, cried as she said goodbye the next morning, and drove the whole way back to Virginia by herself. I wonder what that drive was like for her.

A couple weeks later, while my mom was at work, my dad hired a moving truck and moved out of the house in a single day. He'd told my little sister ahead of time and asked her to go with him and she said yes. He took half the furniture in the house. When mom left for work that morning, she'd had no idea what was about to happen. Though she had talked about divorce a few years earlier, it still took her by surprise. Just like that, her husband and all her girls were gone. For the first time in decades, my mom was alone in an empty house.

She called my dorm room almost every night, crying. Sometimes I was compassionate and strong for her; other times I became impatient and irritated, lecturing her or trying to get off the phone as soon as possible. I remember that old tan dorm-room phone, its crooked curly cord, how I'd press and pull at it to try to make the spiral intact again. How it would always curl back wrong, in a way that felt like an attack.

The divorce took years. Dad complained that Mom was trying to take all his money. He claimed that she was a negligent parent and that he did the bulk of the housework. One of my older sisters showed up in court to refute that and take my mom's side. My dad asked me to write a letter he could use in court defending him. As a teen, I'd always favored my dad, and I wrote an impassioned letter naming all the ways he'd been a superior parent and the times my mom had forgotten to pick me up from rehearsal.

In the end, Dad lost the financial battle. I didn't realize this until years later when Dad offhandedly mentioned something about not being able to retire yet because half his savings were gone. "Gone?" I asked. "But what about the letter I wrote for you in court?"

He sighed. "I didn't end up using it," he said, "because I didn't want your mom to hate you."

———

Over a decade later, I starred in *Fresh Off the Boat*. Fame threw my life into a tailspin. I didn't know how to handle the public scrutiny and I took it out on my mom. Paranoia and anxiety made me say regretful things to her. At a breaking point, I stopped talking to her. Blocked her from my phone and email. For five years, we didn't speak. Only my sisters and close childhood friends knew about this. I never spoke of those years of estrangement because I was afraid of judgment. It's uncomfortable when complete strangers feel entitled to opinions about your personal life. Being known without being *known* . . . it makes a sharp, flailing feeling rise in my chest. Even when I receive positive press, the type of happiness that it produces is a manic, paranoid kind—

there's no relief in it. In fame, even the simple joy of personal accomplishment warps into a circus of noise, drowning out anything tender or beautiful.

Because I played a strong-willed immigrant mother on television, the subject of my own mother came up a lot in interviews. When I did an interview for the *New Yorker* a few years ago, the journalist, also an Asian American woman, refused to believe that my mom wasn't a tiger mom like hers had been. I told her Mom was whimsical and fun. That she never tried to control me; that she gave me freedom. "No way!" replied the journalist. "You mean she wasn't hard on you?" I shook my head nope. She gave me a skeptical look, like I'd just told her that my poop *honest to God* smelled like roses. My answer didn't fit her narrative. Later, she found a quote from someone to confirm her suspicions about my mother: Eddie Huang, the son of the real-life character I played on TV. In her interview with him, Eddie talked about his own mother—how she was hard on him, and that she was his first "hater." Then he implied that our struggles with our mothers were the same. The truth is, Eddie has never met my mom. Never talked to her on the telephone. He doesn't even know her name.

I know he *feels* like he knows her. He's said as much— that my TV portrayal of his mother is so accurate that there's no way I don't share the same personal experience with my own mother. Even though I've always refuted this, he never seemed to hear or believe me. It's something I get a lot. . . .

Everyone, even Asians—*especially* Asians—want my mom to fit into a familiar box. Interviewers ask me:

"Who did you base the character of Jessica Huang on?"

"I based her on the real Jessica Huang," I reply.

"Oh . . . you didn't base her on your own mom? Your mom wasn't like Jessica? She wasn't a tiger mom?"

"Nope."

"Not even a little bit?"

"Nope."

"So, what's she like?"

I know what they want me to say. The non-Asian journalists want a tidy, familiar trope. The Asian journalists want a warm mirror of communal experience. And everybody wants it in a sound bite. But the story of my mom doesn't fit in a sound bite.

I want to tell them about how her smile lit up a room. Or about when she fought to get me my first movie audition, and how she surprised me with it. I want them to see her teaching her daughters to squeeze their butts while dancing ballet. I want to talk about the duck she named Kramer and how gleefully she laughed at *Seinfeld*. How she taught me what a lazy Susan was and how to make chrysanthemums bloom bigger. I want to show pictures of how beautiful she was, how beautifully she used to dress. I want people to know that my fifth-grade teacher, Mrs. Murray, said she was the most beautiful woman she'd ever seen. I want to talk about how she broke us into unfinished mansions and told us to claim our rooms. She was the number one most beautiful girl at the Number One Girls High School. There was so much she could have been. When I imagine her possible life, the life she could have had if she had never married my dad, if she had stayed in Taiwan, if she hadn't built a family and had built herself instead, my mother could have had a mansion of a life.

But I know they won't get it because, like that journalist from the *New Yorker*, they don't want to. They want something that fits their own narrative or something that's a little easier to digest. So instead, I smile and say, "My mother is whimsical."

I don't know why interviewers never ask about my dad.

He and I have always had a good relationship. My dad has never let me down, not once. He's never hurt my feelings, never pressured me to be anything other than exactly who I am. But maybe that's only because I always accepted him as he is, whereas I spent a long time judging my mom. A few years after the divorce, Dad remarried a wonderful woman. She's very different from my mom. Like my dad, she is quiet and gentle. Introverted. They love each other. He's retired now but he still reads biology journals and clones orchids and grows mushrooms for fun. He moves a little slower these days and his eyesight has weakened—he can't shoot a spider from across the room with a rubber band anymore— but he's still the person I feel safest with in the world.

In the middle of the 2020 pandemic, I had a baby girl of my own. During my pregnancy, I decided it was time to reconcile with Mom. I was nervous. What if she wouldn't forgive me or accept me back or, worse—what if she didn't even care? My little sister (who's always been better with my mom) helped us navigate the slow road to reconciliation. We took it day by day. Mom still lives in Virginia, and this was during the height of the COVID pandemic, so it was all via Zooms and FaceTime calls. At first there were a lot of emotions. Joy and pride and relief. Apathy or numbness. Some calls where she acted like the past five years hadn't happened at all. And then on one call she blew up.

"Do you know how embarrassing it is to tell someone your own daughter won't talk to you?" she cried, her eyes full of fury and blame. Her face red, her voice a high-pitched tremor, she began hurling insults at me.

I took a breath and listened to her. It had taken me a while, but I'd learned to be less defensive. And I knew not to ruin an apology with an excuse. After giving her space for all her feelings, I said, "I'm really sorry. I'm sorry I put you through that." She started to calm down, and I continued, "You didn't deserve that, and I know it must have been awful for you and that is on me, and I am sorry."

Suddenly the anger in her throat released, spilling into tears. It hadn't been anger after all; just hurt in disguise. After a few more tears, she fanned her hand in front of her body a few times as if to air out the room. "Ah well! Never mind," she said, forgiving me. "Let me show you my garden!" she exclaimed, taking the iPad outside. We now have a standing FaceTime every Sunday. She usually just wants to show me the flowers in her garden.

Recently, I tried, again, to ask my mom about the story of her and my dad. I needed to hear her side of it. This time, she told me.

"I had to do an internship in college, and I worked in the lab across from his. I knew he liked me because he would just stare at me, all the time. But your dad, he was so quiet. He barely talked to me; I barely knew him. Because ya know, I'm an extrovert and he is an introvert. He didn't even listen to the music I liked! Then my internship was complete, and I left the lab and went back to my college. Two months later your dad came to my dorm—I didn't even know he was coming! He brought a box of mangoes from his family farm and waited downstairs for hours, hoping to see me. Hours he waited! When he finally saw me, he gave me the mangoes—oh, they were the most delicious mangoes—and shyly told me he was going to America to get his PhD. And that's it. He just came to tell me that. Then he left. I was like . . . okay? Good for you? I mean, I barely knew him, he was so quiet! And then, you know, I didn't talk to him for a whole year. Then later when my mom was pressuring me to get married, I thought of him, and I decided to marry him."

Bracing for what would come next, I took a deep breath

and said, "Dad told me that he wrote to you every week for a whole year, and you ignored his letters. You never wrote him back." I was worried that she'd be upset by that, that it would make her seem like the villain I'd judged her to be. But she wasn't upset at all.

"Yes! He did, haha. Yes, that's true, I never wrote him back." She smiled. "Why would I? He was in love with me, but I barely knew him." She shrugged.

The conversation was so easy, why had I feared it? "Mom, can I tell you the story he told me? Will you tell me if I got it right?" I asked her. For some reason, I started feeling giggly.

"Okay, sure," Mom said. The giggles began to catch her too, but we both held back.

"Well. He said you were the most beautiful girl in the world."

"Oh, yes, that part is true!" She nodded, smiling. I laughed. Oh, Mom! "That's why you're so pretty too. All my girls are!"

"He said that after a year of silence, he got a letter from you saying that you two should get married . . ." Before, I always assumed that she'd deny this. That she'd accuse me of always taking my dad's side. But instead, she laughed, seemed surprised I knew the story.

"Yes, that's true too!"

At this point, it felt so freeing to have these truths come out and not be painful for her, that I *really* started giggling.

"Hey! Why are you smiling? It wasn't like that; it wasn't

romantic! Don't get all dreamy!" she insisted, mistaking my giggles for swoons. "There was no love!"

And here I'd thought she would be too ashamed to admit that she never loved him. "Oh, I know it wasn't that! It's just . . . I always thought, like . . . I dunno . . . Mom, maybe did you have a boyfriend before him? And maybe you wrote that marriage letter impulsively after a breakup?"

I could tell she hadn't thought about that for a long time, and as it started coming back to her, I could see that I'd been right!

"I had this job, at a trading company. I didn't know how to type. Or—well, I knew how, but back then it was typewriters and if you made one mistake the whole letter was ruined. I hated that job, so I quit and then my mom said, 'What are you going to do now?' She was in Japan with my father because he had a stroke, so I had to take care of my brother, who would ask me every night, 'What are you making me for dinner?'

"And there was this boy I loved and I was so upset over him when he broke my heart. Then my mom was pressuring me about what I was going to do after I quit my job. I didn't really love your dad. I just thought . . . oh well, I don't know what I was thinking. I was so full of heartache I wasn't thinking straight."

Just like I'd been with George.

"Did you sleep with that first boyfriend?"

"Oh come on! Of course not! You know, my generation, if you even held hands, you were basically engaged. So

I thought that's what we were. But then he didn't want to be with me anymore. Oh! I was so upset. I would just wander the streets crying."

I started laughing, overcome with relief and joy. "Mom! I knew it! That's totally how I imagined it! You were being impulsive, trying to run away from the pain!"

"Yes, that's it!" She began laughing too, surprised I understood. "Impulsive! Anything to get away! But you know, I loved being in Taiwan. I didn't really want to go to America. I was popular in Taiwan! So, then your dad, he actually came, I was so surprised, and I had to tell him the truth. I told him I didn't really love him, that I didn't mean any of it, that I probably wouldn't ever love him, so that maybe he shouldn't get married to me . . . but then he still wanted to marry me! I don't know why! In fact, he said we *had* to—he had spent all his savings on the flight—so I felt bad, and I married him. Then he went back to the States, and I was supposed to follow a month later. But then I wrote him a letter saying 'I think this was a mistake. I don't think I should come to America.' And then he said, 'Okay. If you really feel that way, then you shouldn't come. But if you don't come, then I will kill myself. Because I spent all my savings on the flights, and I can't face my adviser and tell him it was all for nothing and that I have no wife anymore.' And I thought, oh no! I can't let him do that," she continued. "So, I guess I just came over, because even though I didn't love him, I didn't want him to *die*." Her smile was practical, as if to say, *duh, of course*. Dad hadn't told me that part. (Later, when I asked him about it, he denied ever saying that to her. *I never said that. I mean . . . yes, we had to wait a month for the visa to go through, but . . . threaten to kill myself? That's like holding someone hostage, I would never do that,* he said, adding, *and I only cried on the flight home because I felt cheated . . . like she lied to me, okay?* I believe both of them. I don't think my dad ever threatened to kill himself. That's not like him. But I also believe that my mom *felt* like my dad would have killed himself if she abandoned him. That she was truly worried about what it would do to him. She's always been a preemptive worrier.)

"Oh, and my mother," Mom continued on the FaceTime, suddenly kissing the sky. "I will forever love my mother for this. Once she got back from Japan, I was already in America and I told her how I made a mistake, how I didn't love your dad. She realized how unhappy I was. So, my mother told your dad she would reimburse him all his savings and money he spent on flights if he let me come back to Taiwan. But then I got pregnant with your sister the first time we had sex, so oh well! Too late! And a marriage based on no love—wow, look! It lasted almost thirty years! Haha! Pretty good, huh?"

We were both giggling at this point, giddy and happy to be connecting with each other. She pointed her finger up in the air in a *eureka* gesture, the same way I also do when I'm making a point. "But look! See? I got four beautiful girls out of it! It all turned out good!" she declared, a huge grin on her face.

"Yeah, Dad told me that too. He told me that it was hard

at first, because you didn't love him, but then once you had a baby it got better, because you loved being a mom."

"Oh yes, that is true." She nodded brightly, smiling with that very specific smile moms have—chin tucked down, eyes tilted up, lips pursed with restraint as if holding back a burst of love. "I loved being a mom."

I didn't have my daughter until I was thirty-eight years old. By that time, I'd already experienced love and loss many times over, established the career of my dreams, bought my fairy-tale house, and was financially secure. When my boyfriend and I drove home from the hospital with our newborn, we both marveled at how calm and ready we felt. We weren't scared. If we'd been younger, it would have been very different. My mom was twenty-two and living in a foreign country when she had her first baby. By twenty-four, she had two babies. My parents didn't even have health insurance. I can't imagine how hard that must have been. But she doesn't seem to regret any of it. "You know why I had FOUR?" my mom asked me, grinning, over FaceTime the other day. "Because I love babies! Now you know too."

Lots of women I know express worry that they are becoming like their mothers. In a way, I feel like I'll never know if I become like her, because she never really got to be herself. Having kids so young changed everything. I feel such guilt about it, sometimes. Like me and my sisters stunted her potential. I know that is the most cliché thing in the world for a daughter to say . . . but it's just that there was so much she could have been. But instead, she broke herself so everyone else could blossom.

When my father first told me the story of how he and my mother married, we were driving down the interstate. It was a gray day, the roads wet, a drizzling mist suspended in the air. I could tell that he was trying to sound angry, but he kept clearing his throat and letting out small coughs, as if to stop something from rising in his throat. As he told me the story, it was a strange new feeling for me—that moment when you realize your parents had entire lives before they had you. I thought of my mother, standing so still, gazing out the windows of those unfinished mansions. And then I saw my father, hands gripped on the steering wheel, staring down the road, unable to look at me. With his voice breaking like a teenage boy's, he said, "You know I still have it—that letter your mom wrote me all those years ago. I still have it."

This past fall, I went back to see the mansions my mother broke us into. It had been over thirty years since last I'd seen them. Back when they were all under construction. Now they were home to families. There were decorative mailboxes, college sports team flags, chalk and tricycles on driveways—hints of the lives inside. The copper dome hadn't turned green, but a rich brown, like tree bark, or an old penny. Driving through the neighborhood, I was stunned. This time, it wasn't the mansions that awed me but the trees! They'd been saplings when last I saw them. Now stately and handsome, they towered higher than I ever would have imagined they could grow. And not just up but out—branching over the streets in fluttering yellow canopies, their slender leaves spiraling down over the car windshield, like golden pinwheels. It was a cold fall day, but I got a warm, tingly feeling in my chest, like a sparkler lit up and firing. Like I had a special secret: I knew what they were before they were mansions. Back when they were just being built. I can still hear the echoes. When two little girls ran wild through empty rooms and hallways, their whole lives ahead of them.

Jumping off the swings at Maybeury Elementary School

Acknowledgments

This book wouldn't exist if it weren't for the patience, support, friendship, and faith of some pretty terrific people.

My wonderful book agent (and fellow Virginian!), Byrd Leavell. Thank you for your support and encouragement. I like everything about you.

Kara Watson, my editor—without your gentle questions, this book would have considerably less grace.

Larry Taube, my manager. People with your level of integrity, taste, and class are hard to find in the entertainment industry, and I am lucky to have you.

Bryna Rifkin and Celena Madlansacay—it's so nice to have publicists who treat me as a person, not a product.

My kickass lawyers for being so thorough with this book: Huy Nguyen, Tom J. Ferber, Michael Niborski, and most especially . . . Steve Warren. Steve, you've been my biggest cheerleader since day one. Love talking books with you, love your passion and your eternally positive attitude.

Jay Shaw for designing an amazing book cover that I never could have even imagined.

The folks who kept my daily life together while I was

writing this: Andrew Meyer, Chelsea McKinnies, Gary Potter, Nicole Dean, Gayle Spitz, Justine Jones, KC Phillips, Alicia Morales, Amy Morales, Luana Costa.

The team at Scribner/S&S: Nan Graham, Elisa Rivlin, Jaya Miceli, Davina Mock-Maniscalco, Dan Cuddy, Katie Monaghan, Abby Novak, Zoey Cole, Brianna Yamashita, Stu Smith, Sabrina Pyun.

Artistic mentors and inspirations: Craig Archibald, Lorene Scafaria, Becki Jones, Jennie Israel, Will Eno, Chris Yogi, Chloe Okuno, and Becky Cole.

My life is better for my friendships and in turn, so is this book. I love and cherish you: Marrianne H., Molly Flynn, Jeffery Ryan Creager, Thea Brooks, Brea Grant, Sean O'Malley, Leah Jackson, Ryan Spindell, Jack Clift, Jacques Belanger, Kimmie Rice, Rachael Taylor, Kit Williamson, John Halbach, T. Justin Ross, Grant McFadden, Mike Griffin, Nora Lum, Jing Lusi, Lyman Creason, Sharon Pinches, Michel deAscentiis, Michael Jack Greenwald, Brett Bietz, Timothy Huang, Chiké Okonkwo, Matt Miller and Bernice Chao.

Special thanks to Ben Hethcoat, Alex Cameron, Miles Kane, John Congleton, Jessica Elbaum, Jimmy O. Yang, Amy Schumer, Mindy Kaling, Jennifer Lopez, Buck, Molly Greenwald, Bridget Brager, Mitchell Travers, Malcolm Barrett, Rachel Khong, B. D. Wong, Rich and Sher Lahvic, Harrison Waterstreet, and Hylda Queally.

Guardian angels above: Betty and Syd Phillips, Therin Brooks, Jim Frizzell, and Lee Slatton.

And saving the best for last—my family. Mom, Dad, M–, Helen, E–, Amy, Gene, Kenn, Johann, Ryan P., Vera W., Micki, Gary, Patrick, and most especially Ryan Kattner and our beautiful daughter.